# Dramatically Honest

How to own your authenticity in the
workplace

# Dramatically Honest

## How to own your authenticity in the workplace

SOPHIE HUSSEY

**GRC** Solutions

GRC Solutions
Unit 3, Clive Court
Bartholomew's Walk
Cambridgeshire Business Park
Ely, Cambridgeshire
CB7 4EA
United Kingdom
*www.itgovernance.co.uk*

First published in the United Kingdom in 2025 by GRC Solutions.

ISBN 978-1-78778-593-9

Cover image originally sourced from Adobe Stock.

# ACKNOWLEDGEMENTS

This book would not have been possible without a small network of people who have empowered and supported me through the process.

First and foremost, to my family: Chris, Niamh, Erin and Ben. Thank you for your support, your patience with my many hours writing in the kitchen and not always being fully present when I was 'in the zone'.

To my brilliant friend Emma, who is my authenticity guru, unapologetically herself and my biggest cheerleader.

I would also like to thank David Barrow and Lucy Grimwade, for their support and helpful feedback during the production of this book.

And lastly, but by no means least, to my wonderful parents: Ann and Geoff. Thank you for a wonderful childhood and instilling in me the core values that give me strength, courage and the audacity to stand out from the crowd.

# FOREWORDS

It is with a great sense of pride and pleasure that I was asked to write this foreword for Sophie.

I met Sophie many years ago while working as a freelance IT consultant for the company where she worked. She appeared to be someone who was comfortable being herself and demonstrated authenticity.

The first time I saw Sophie, like the Miss Marple of the IT department and as the head of service management, she was heading over to my side of the office to investigate why a change hadn't worked, or something was broken – the details don't matter. What does matter is she was unashamedly herself, making enquiries with the service desk team about the issue and the plan for restoring service. Her experienced professionalism, combined with a slightly teasing yet firm manner left no casual observer in any doubt who was in charge.

In my three years with the company I had the opportunity to watch her work and see the positive impact she was having on the company and those around her. She always led with enthusiasm and passion for her role and her team, while also striving to elevate those around her and champion their achievements. The home baked goods she would regularly bring into the office to share with her colleagues also helped!

Since leaving the company we both reconnected some years later during a difficult time in both our personal lives and since then I've had the pleasure of watching her flourish and grow even more. I'm now pleased to call her my girlfriend, partner in crime – and as she likes to say, 'her person'.

So why is this book important? I think there are many reasons why, and there is so much to take away from this book, but for me there are two main reasons this book deserves your time:

- **Being your authentic self is hard.** This is especially true in the modern world with constant pressures from social media, challenges around your identity (whether that be your gender or other factors), and an increasingly uncertain and multi-polar world where opinions are often divisive and extreme.
- **Being a woman in tech.** Sadly this is still fraught with challenges in a very male dominated industry. In my experience organisations and projects I've been involved with that included a broad mix of men and women, with varying levels of experience and diverse backgrounds, were always the best places to work.

Sophie gets right into these challenges and more with a very straightforward and unapologetically authentic approach. She guides the reader on how to be authentic using stories and experiences form her own life and career in a very real and unvarnished way.

Sophie has significant experience and credentials that enable her to thoroughly explore authenticity in this context. With over 2 decades of experience as a woman in tech, including being a lifelong coach and mentor, she brings a wealth of eye-opening stories about her successes, failures and lessons learned along the way.

Sophie regularly speaks at multiple industry leading conferences and events, challenging her boundaries and promoting her authentic self. She is also a 5 x Women in Tech awards nominee, being shortlisted on four occasions.

Through her coaching and mentoring of clients and colleagues including people recommended to her by peers, she has consistently put her words into action, advocating for and promoting everyone to find their authentic self.

While this book in many ways is a step-by-step guide to finding and developing your authentic self, you can open this book on practically any page and take something away or learn something new. I was especially drawn to the chapter on values, and how this forms part of who you are and your authentic self. It never occurred to me that thinking about and understanding your values was such an important part of your authenticity and how you must reevaluate this over time. I found this book challenged me to think deeply about my values and what being authentic really means – and I hope you do too.

**Chris Jackson**

**VP of research**

There's a quietly profound strength in someone who decides to share their truth, not the refined, practised version but the genuine, raw, beautifully chaotic one. That's exactly what Sophie Hussey accomplishes in *Dramatically Honest – How to own your authenticity in the workplace*. In doing so, Sophie crafts something far beyond a mere book.

This work intertwines memoir, manifesto, and a compelling call to action.

Sophie doesn't simply reflect on her journey; she immerses us deeply in it. Through a mix of personal narratives, real-world statistics, and grounded insights, Sophie encourages us to re-evaluate what authenticity truly means. Not as a fleeting hashtag trend or leadership buzzword, but as a conscious and courageous daily practice.

Sophie addresses feelings many of us face but rarely articulate: the pressure to conform, the fear of being perceived as "too much," and the draining effort it demands to belong in environments that may not embrace diversity that veers too far away from the everyday norm.

By acknowledging the discomfort and resistance, this book guides us toward growth with a comforting and confronting clarity.

If you've ever felt the need to tone yourself down to fit in…

If you've ever wondered about your place at the table…

If you've ever just needed someone to tell you "you're not alone", this book is for you.

It's authentic. It's heartfelt. And above all, it's human.

As you delve into the book and reach its conclusion, you will find yourself standing a bit taller, speaking a bit louder, and ultimately, showing up as your true self.

Because what Sophie reveals to us is blindingly obvious yet so difficult to achieve as we struggle with everyday tension. In this book you'll find that the help, guidance and experiences shared by Sophie will provide you with the desire and impetus to be what you want to be, or in Sophie's words:

*"Be bold, be brave, be you!"*

**David Barrow**

**Co-author of *Allyship Actually – Why it's 'We' and not 'Me'***

# ABOUT THE AUTHOR

Hi! I am Sophie. Thank you for reading my book and joining me on this exploration and journey of authenticity. Before we dive in, please allow me to introduce myself.

I am from a town called Aylesbury in Buckinghamshire, which is about 40 miles north of London. I grew up on the 'wrong' side of town compared to my classmates, which meant my social standing at school was not particularly high, often resulting in bullying from my peers and even from some teachers. I bore this all internally, not sharing my experiences with my parents. I survived school and college with a smile, often a sarcastic retort and a belief that one day I would find my people as well as a sense of belonging.

I grew up with my mum, stepdad, brother, stepbrother and stepsister. Despite not coming from a financially affluent family, I had a rich childhood with many laughs and adventures along the way. I have a few more siblings on my father's side, one of whom is in my list of top five favourite people of all time and who lives in Canada, living her best life being an all-round brilliant human.

I moved to Yorkshire in my early twenties and have two daughters (Niamh and Erin), who are at college and university. I am a single parent and have been for a long time, which is possibly the toughest role I will ever have fulfilled. It is not easy filling both parental roles at the same time – being 'fun Mum' while maintaining boundaries is like pushing opposing magnets together or pushing water uphill with a fork. However, I am incredibly proud of what I have achieved with two fantastic humans, who will be excellent additions to society.

My partner and I have been together for a few years, and it is his encouragement that gave me the extra courage I needed to start my own business – something for which I will be eternally grateful. I am also lucky enough to have acquired a stepson in the last few years and try to channel the parenting approach my stepdad took with me and my brother, by being an ally, a friend and a constant supporter.

Overall, as an individual, I believe in random acts of kindness, leading with empathy and, while far from perfect, I try to be the best person I can be. I am an introvert in an extrovert's job and am incredibly shy, but have honed the skill to compartmentalise, driving myself forward in my career.

My experience is from nearly 25 years of working in a male-dominated environment. Certainly, early on, there were challenges that needed careful navigation. There have been times where I have felt that I had to make myself small, times where I have stood my ground and times where I thought showing my full self was going to have career-limiting results.

I started my career working on an IT service desk and followed a technical path as an infrastructure and telephony engineer until becoming a service desk manager. Then I followed a service management path, ending in being the head of service management and, unofficially, a deputy chief information officer (CIO) in the financial sector.

My role became redundant in early 2022 and I took a leap of faith, backing myself in starting my own consultancy business, Lapis Consulting Services Ltd. The company is in its fourth year of trading and I absolutely love being my own boss, engaging with clients and further expanding my skillset.

I have been a mentor for the majority of my career. I do this because I want to pay it forward, supporting the growth of others on their own journey. I also volunteer as a science, technology, engineering and mathematics (STEM) ambassador, where I go into schools and colleges to help support future generations on their career journeys, sharing the fact that there are more career pathways open to them, particularly in technology, than they may be aware of.

For years, women have been labelled: too emotional, too dramatic, too much. Like many women, I've felt the weight of the stereotypes that try to shrink us: the idea that we're less logical, more reactive, harder to lead, and so on. I've spent my life pushing back on those. What I've learned is that honesty – raw, clear, and unfiltered – isn't a flaw. It's power. The title "Dramatically Honest" flips the script. It's a wink at the stereotype, not a submission to it. This book isn't dramatic, it's honest. And that's exactly the point.

# CONTENTS

# Contents

# Contents

# CHAPTER 1: INTRODUCTION – WHAT IS AUTHENTICITY?

Welcome to the journey of breaking down the barriers to being authentic as a woman in technology. Let us start off by saying that you do not need to be a woman in tech for this book to be useful. It has been written from the stance of a woman working in a male-dominated industry, but the challenges faced are not solely experienced by women, and the barriers to being authentic at work can be universal.

In all honesty, the areas we will go through in this book are applicable to anyone working in an environment that is dominated by a characteristic that they do not have, or for those who are searching for the confidence to be who they are at work. So, if you are flicking through this and wondering whether to pick it up, ask yourself this question:

"Am I truly myself at work or do I dampen who I am to satisfy my surroundings?"

If the answer is that you are not truly yourself at work, then this book is for you!

**Be bold, be brave, be you!**

The fact that you are reading this book is a fantastic step on the path to finding the courage to be yourself in the workplace, and in other areas of your life. It is not an easy thing to do, breaking out from the mould. We live in a world that is more connected than at any other time in history yet there is a distance through the interaction with technology, and, of course, there are societal and cultural pressures to conform. It is these pressures that can result in a feeling of disconnection or of not belonging. Certainly, this is something that inspired me to write this book, to discover a way to belong and to connect without sacrificing my own identity and values.

It is important to remember as you are working your way through the chapters that what works for one person may not work for you. The advice and guidance is exactly that – information that is being imparted to allow you to make decisions and choices from a base of knowledge and experience. There may be times where you are inspired to take action in the same way as described in the stories, which is fantastic, so long as you ensure you are doing it in a way that is true to who YOU are. If a course of action is not aligned with your values and beliefs, then taking that action may not be authentically you – but more on that later.

**Structure of the book**

The book is broken into chapters to work through the idea of authenticity. They are designed to take you on a journey from understanding what being authentic means to focusing on the practical applications of how to be you at work.

Within each chapter is a story that adds a real-life example of a barrier being met. Not all stories result in a happy ending where the goal of being authentic is realised, but from each story, there is a lesson that was learned. Please note that in the interest of privacy, some of the names and locations in the stories may have been changed, but the events and conversations have not; what you read is what happened from the author's perspective.

Throughout the book, you will find a block of text, like the following, which is a hint, tip or trick that you can use to support you on your journey.

> **Hint:**
>
> As with any journey, you need to adapt it to fit your needs. If you need a break, have one. If you need to skip to the next part, then do it.

At the back of the book is an appendix, which has a wealth of resources that you can use to support you on your journey as well as opportunities for further reading, self-study and development.

**How to use the book**

There are several ways to approach this book:

1. Read it from cover to cover, following the typical journey of a book.
2. Review the chapters and subheadings, and jump to the section of the book that is most relevant.
3. Skip straight to the stories of real-life events that explain how I approached various situations.

Whatever approach YOU choose to take, that is the right one. This book has been written to support you, help you on your journey, and give you some tips on how best to bring your true self into the workplace.

**What is authenticity?**

What do you think it looks like to be 'authentic'? Is it in the way someone dresses? The way they do their hair? They way they speak or the accent they have? The things that they do or achieve? Or the things that they say? It reminds me of my favourite interview question to ask candidates, where I ask them what professionalism looks like. Is there one thing that defines 'professionalism'? No. There are many characteristics of professionalism and the same applies to what 'authentic' looks like.

Let us start with what the word 'authentic' means and where it comes from.

The Oxford English Dictionary definition of 'authentic' is:

> *"authentic, adj. & n.*
> *Definition: Genuine; not feigned or false. Now the usual sense. Of a document, artefact, artwork, etc:"*

The keyword from this definition is "genuine" or, to put it another way, "not feigned or false".

Let us see how AI would define being authentic. This is what ChatGPT said in September 2024:

> *"Being authentic means being genuine, true to oneself, and consistent in one's actions, beliefs, and values. It involves:*
>
> 1. ***Self-Awareness****: Understanding your own emotions, motivations, and values.*
>
> 2. ***Honesty****: Communicating and acting in ways that reflect your true thoughts and feelings.*
>
> 3. ***Integrity****: Aligning your behaviour with your principles and values, even in the face of external pressures.*
>
> 4. ***Consistency****: Maintaining the same persona and values in different contexts and over time.*
>
> 5. ***Transparency****: Being open about your intentions and not hiding behind false pretences.*

*Authenticity fosters trust and builds deeper, more meaningful relationships, both personally and professionally."*

Combining the two definitions from the dictionary and from generative AI, you get a picture of what 'authentic' really means. It is about being true, real, honest, transparent – the combination of positive values and attributes that makes something or someone trustworthy.

Let us throw in an analogy here to bring this to life and think about consumer goods and their authenticity. There are a variety of items you can buy that will come with a certificate of authenticity (art, jewellery, etc.). This certificate verifies that the item is real, its origins can be trusted and the value associated with it is accurate. If you have ever sold clothing on Vinted or eBay, it is normal to have to provide evidence of the branding or authenticity. Providing multiple photos of the labels of a Nike sweatshirt, to show that it is genuine and worth the amount of money you are selling it for, is commonplace to prove authenticity. You would not buy an Aston Martin or Porsche from a newspaper advertisement without checking its logbook papers were correct. The last thing you would want to do is buy an elite sports car that upon closer inspection was a mid-size family car!

If only certificates of authenticity were available for people, it would make this a whole lot easier!

## Being authentic in a Disney movie

I am a sucker for an animated Disney movie and when watching *Encanto* recently, I felt it was the perfect analogy for being authentic. Why? Well, for those who have not seen it, the premise is a family who are blessed with gifts of magic that are given to each family member when they come of age.

These gifts include super strength, super hearing, the ability to transfigure, to heal, etc. The main character in the film does not receive a magical gift when she comes of age and struggles to find her place in the family. She struggles to understand what her strengths are and what unique qualities she can bring to the family.

When things start to go wrong for her relatives, the heroine sets out to find the cause of the problem and why the magic is failing. She learns that some members of the family who do have a gift do not feel as though they can truly be themselves and that they have got to live up to the expectations of their grandmother. Members of the family are in essence not being truly authentic in order to meet the expectations of those around them. In doing so, they are hiding who they truly are, which ultimately impacts the magic that surrounds them.

Spoiler alert if you have not seen the film... What saves the magic is each member of the family embracing who they are, bringing their authentic self to the surface, all of the time. For example, being super strong and helping people while also taking a break and allowing themselves to be looked after too, or not having a special gift whilst being the glue that holds the family together.

**How to be authentic**

How to be 'authentic' will differ from person to person, but the essence is to hold true to who you are. It involves displaying values that allow others to recognise an individual who is confident in their self-awareness, is honest, conscientious, dedicated (or whichever other values they are showing), which ultimately makes that individual trustworthy and a person to respect. And this is the key.

We will just highlight some keywords here:

- Trustworthiness
- Honesty
- Respect
- Self-awareness

These words are all things that interlink when it comes to being authentic. Realistically, in the workplace, if your colleagues/peers/managers can see these attributes in you, this is a positive. Most importantly, perhaps, seeing these attributes in yourself is the key to success, to building self-confidence, to being who you truly are in the workplace and not being afraid to do so.

Being authentic does not stem from waking up one morning and deciding, "Today, I'm going to bring my true self to the forefront." It stems from understanding who you are, what makes you tick, your drivers, your passions, your interests and your beliefs. All the facets of you that form your sense of humour, your personality, your identity, etc. are built on the foundations of your values and are the external display of your authentic self.

# CHAPTER 2: BARRIERS TO AUTHENTICITY

> Barriers to being yourself, obstacles that may give you pause and prevent you from embracing yourself. We may not be able to stop barriers from existing, but we can certainly understand them. To know them better will allow you to find ways to overcome them.

I would not need to write this book if being authentic at work was not a challenge, so let us spend a bit of time talking about these barriers. Whether it is when you are faced with your own imposter syndrome or whether you work somewhere that is not a psychologically safe environment, we will walk through those things that can be difficult to navigate.

We will start with generic barriers and then look at any additional barriers that may exist for women in the workplace.

## General barriers

### *Fear of rejection*

This may seem like the most obvious barrier to being your authentic self and I suspect you are right. Next are some examples of sources talking about the fear of rejection, what it means, and working to understand the multitude of factors that cause people to fear rejection.

- Medical News Today (2024)[1] – talks about the fear of rejection, what it is and how to overcome it.
- Psychology Today (2019)[2] – explains the pain of social rejection.
- NeuroscienceNews.com (2022)[3] – discusses the need to understand and reframe the fear of rejection.

The fear of rejection is a universal experience for people regardless of the setting they are in, so it is no surprise that it is a barrier to being authentic in the workplace.

Think about it: you are starting a new job and it is the weekend before you walk into the office and meet your new colleagues. The only interaction you have had with people there so far has been through the recruitment process with the hiring manager (maybe some other people in the organisation associated with the process, but limited interaction with people who work there). Your first proper engagement with your colleagues is going to be on that first day, so you are likely prepping what you are going to wear, considering what to do about lunch (do you take a homemade lunch or do you go empty-handed in case one of the team wants to go for lunch with you), considering how you will greet your team (handshakes or a smile and wave), and so on.

Now ask yourself why you are considering all those things. Is it because you want to make a good impression? Let us dig a little deeper: why do you want to make a good impression?

---

[1] *https://www.medicalnewstoday.com/articles/fear-of-rejection.*

[2] *https://www.psychologytoday.com/us/blog/the-modern-heart/201906/5-reasons-why-social-pain-is-real.*

[3] *https://neurosciencenews.com/rejection-fear-20892/.*

Most likely because you want to fit in and have a positive work environment. And what is the worst thing that could happen? You walk in on your first day, accidentally say or do the wrong thing, resulting in making a fool of yourself or your new colleagues not liking you. It may not be an out-and-out rejection, but it is a rejection, nonetheless.

The degree to which you feel a fear of rejection will be different for everyone and will be linked to a whole host of factors. (Enter the psychology world!). Regardless of the degree to which you are impacted by the fear of rejection, it can be a blocker to being authentic at work.

### *Lack of self-awareness and low self-esteem*

Not everyone has the gift of self-awareness. This could be because they have not taken the time for self-reflection or perhaps they exist in a world that is so domineering (the people, the environment, etc.) that they do not really know who they are (this could be cultural, societal, etc.). It can be difficult to be truly authentic if you do not know what your values, needs, desires and objectives are.

> **Tip:**
> **Not everyone has the gift of self-awareness.**

People can have low self-esteem when they are struggling with their own worth and value, when they feel as though they cannot be true to themselves. This may lead to them adopting behaviours, values or roles that they think will make them more appealing to others. They will perhaps find a level of acceptance even if it is at the cost of being true to themselves.

This barrier can be closely linked to the next one in the list, as well as linked to mental health and well-being as a barrier to authenticity.

### *Social conditioning, cultural or societal pressures and expectations*

Sadly, we still live in a world where some believe there are jobs only suitable for men or for women, in the same way that there are pink toys for girls and blue for boys. There is evidence of a 'pink tax'[4] on some products for women, including prices of up to 40% more on toiletries for women than those for men (according to research by The Co-operative Bank in an article in 2024)[5], just because the products are pink. This is also something that has been discussed during UK Parliament sessions.[6]

The fact is that we are conditioned from an early age to accept societal and cultural 'norms' and if, or when, we question that status quo, it can be not only divisive but also isolating. Stepping out from the crowd to push boundaries and question the way it has always been is a daunting proposition and one that takes courage.

When you consider this in the context of the workplace, you are faced with questions. For example, what if there are expectations from the organisation to behave in a particular way? I do not mean in terms of the values that the organisation has defined for itself, but what if the company

---

[4] *https://now.org/blog/the-pink-tax-the-cost-of-being-a-woman/.*

[5] *https://www.co-operativebank.co.uk/content-hub/articles-and-advice/pink-tax-women-paying-more-for-their-essentials/.*

[6] *https://edm.parliament.uk/early-day-motion/55690/pink-tax.*

is led with a very outdated or old-fashioned view on who does what, what is acceptable for people to discuss in the workplace and the way they deliver the message, etc.? If you are concerned about job security, how you are perceived in the workplace and whether that may lead to career-limiting consequences, then being your authentic self may be both daunting and a risk you are not prepared to take.

### *Perfectionism and a lack of vulnerability*

How many of you have been asked the interview question "what are your strengths and weaknesses" and answered that being a perfectionist is one of your weaknesses? It is a stock answer and true for many people. But what does it mean to be 'a perfectionist' in relation to being your authentic self?

Maybe another question here is, what does it mean if you are not perfect? To open yourself to anything less than being 'the best' means allowing vulnerability to enter the room. To admit that perhaps you, like everyone, are flawed. In the workplace, there are many concerns and anxieties that may exist in relation to being flawed, such as the following:

- What will my colleagues think of me?
- What will my boss think of me?
- Will I get passed over for promotion because I am not perfect?
- Will I get a terrible rating in my annual performance review?
- Will I be considered weak or ineffective?
- Will my future career be impacted?

This is quite a complex thought process and realistically, it may seem easier to follow the curve and bend yourself to fit a mould that you consider to be more acceptable where you work.

Just to be clear here, striving for perfection does not automatically mean that you are placing a barrier between yourself and being who you truly are in the workplace. Striving for excellence and delivering high-quality work is something to take pride in. That is, providing you recognise that perfection is an ideal, not a reality, and certainly not when striving for this ideal comes at the cost of allowing yourself to be you.

> **Tip:**
>
> **Ask yourself this, "What does it mean if I am NOT perfect?"**

### *Toxic relationships/leadership/environments and a pressure to succeed*

There are organisations that are not harmonious and well led. I am sure this will come as a shock to many.

That was a joke.

Unless you are incredibly lucky, it is likely that you will have worked in an environment that was not great, and you have wondered why you worked there. The workplace could have been unsatisfactory for a number of reasons, such as:

- There was a lack of psychological safety – things were not allowed to fail or there was a blame culture.
- There was a pressure to succeed – everything needed to be delivered on time, with no issues, with the expectation of working long hours to achieve this.

- The environment was cliquey – if you were not 'in the club', you were not likely to progress in your career, but to be in the 'club', you had to fit a certain image or 'type'.
- The leadership led by fear and/or disruption – leading by example is not always something that those in power within an organisation take into account or even care about.

A work environment that is not psychologically safe is not typically the breeding ground for authenticity. The pressure to conform, deliver or act in a particular way to avoid negative attention can override the will or ability to be who you really are when you are in such an environment.

### *Mental-health challenges*

As with low self-esteem, there are also mental-health challenges to consider when it comes to the things that can hold someone back from being themselves generally and at work. For example, anxiety, depression or trauma can alter the way we see ourselves and also impact whether we feel safe expressing ourselves and ultimately being authentic.

For any reader who is struggling with their mental health, there is a wealth of support and information available, from sources such as (web links are in the appendix):

- Mind;
- Samaritans; and
- ANDYSMANCLUB.

> **Tip:**
> **Remember, it is okay to not be okay.**

# CHAPTER 3: BARRIERS FOR WOMEN IN THE WORKPLACE

> Beyond the general barriers, there are those that exist specifically for women and any minority group. Here, we delve into what they are and the challenges they bring. Knowing and recognising these will support your journey of authenticity.

Some of the barriers for women in the workplace are linked to general barriers, such as the pressure to conform (linked to social conditioning, cultural or societal pressures and expectations).

Let us get straight to the point, call it as it is and open the doors to some home truths. This section may make some readers feel uncomfortable. We are going to talk about some of the challenges and factors that contribute to inequality in the world we live in that impact women in the workplace. Some of you will read this nodding along, recognising how these factors impact you in your working life. Some of you will be allies and will nod along having learned from female colleagues how these things exist in their world. And some of you will be reading this as totally new information – and may even disagree! It is going to be eye-opening.

## Gender bias and stereotyping

Before we get into the detail of how gender bias and stereotyping is a barrier to authenticity, let us make sure we understand the definition of the term. The Cambridge Dictionary definition[7] is below:

> "***gender bias, noun***
>
> *definition: unfair difference in the way women and men are treated"*

Now, we will move into how this can be a barrier to authenticity.

Imagine you are a young woman in an organisation where the ratio of men to women in technology roles is somewhere in the region of 10:1. You are applying for an internal technical role in an infrastructure team where there is a minimum level of training and expertise required to be considered for the role, with some desirable qualifications listed, too. You have the expected level of training and expertise to be considered for the role.

There are five people competing for the role – four men and you. The company has a history of promoting men into more senior technical roles, with any female positions typically being in human resources (HR), administrative and customer-facing roles. The hiring manager is known for recruiting male candidates to his team, as seen in comments he makes like "they're not emotional like women" and "men are just more logical" and "women are better at organising and admin work, whereas men are doers and crack on".

This is not the first time you have applied for the role. In fact, it is the third time, and previously, you have missed out on the promotion as the position has gone to a male member of the team who does not have the required qualifications and

---

[7] *https://dictionary.cambridge.org/dictionary/english/gender-bias.*

is junior in terms of experience and approach. You have prepped for the interview. You have spoken to the other colleagues in the team to get a feel for what a typical day looks like, and you have done your research. Not only do you have all the required qualifications, but you are also studying for further accreditations to support you in your career. But what you also have is ovaries, which are a potential blocker when it comes to the hiring manager – particularly based on the comments he has openly made in the office.

Do you think gender bias is in play here?

Yes. And this is one of the more blatant examples.

Exploring gender bias and stereotyping a little further, women often report that they find themselves being perceived as too soft or gentle in the workplace or the opposite, being considered too tough and a 'ball-buster'. Finding the balance between these two can be difficult and result in women suppressing qualities that allow them to be their authentic selves, dampening down the empathy and dialling down the assertiveness to avoid negative reactions when they do not conform to the stereotypes, or when they conform too much, such as:

- Women are naturally maternal, nurturing and expected to be in care-giving roles.
- Women in high-powered roles are controlling, difficult and bossy.
- Women are overly emotional, irrational and make decisions based on how they feel rather than on facts.

I can bring this to life with a personal example of gender stereotyping from something that happened several years ago.

A meeting was held with colleagues from another team who needed to be held to account for unauthorised changes that had resulted in a series of major incidents, negatively impacting external customers. Some of my team were attending the meeting and we had discussed the session ahead of time to talk about the approach and desirable outcomes. I chaired the meeting and let rip, Sophie-style. When I say "let rip", what I mean is that I calmly and professionally held the parties to account, expressed my disappointment in their unilateral actions and asked for a clear set of actions to avoid the issue reoccurring. My approach is always to be polite yet firm, not raising my voice but using tone and inflection to express myself. Ensuring that everyone fully understands my position and what that means for them.

The meeting ended with everyone knowing the next steps and with an agreed understanding on what positive behaviours and outcomes would be expected going forward. Importantly, it was also highlighted what the penalty for repeat offences would be should similar incidents occur in the future. It had not been a meeting with shouting, berating or telling people off in a way that would denote a parent-child relationship, rather than a professional relationship.

On the walk back to my desk, one of my team members said to me, "I thought you were going to give them hell. You were far too soft in there." I was somewhat surprised that this was how my approach to the meeting and the situation had been perceived by one of my team. The expectation from them was that I should have shouted, ranted and raved, demanding outcomes and a change in behaviours. What is interesting here, however, is that in a similar meeting run by one of my male peers who took the same approach where my team member was present, he did not comment after that meeting to say the male leader was "too soft" but in fact, he left the meeting making comments about having felt he had been told off and reprimanded.

### The pressure to conform fuelled by a fear of judgement or backlash

There is an unrealistic expectation among many people that you need to be friends with everyone you work with. While this is usually not possible, the critical focus for everyone should be in fostering a friendly and supportive environment where everyone feels heard and included – irrespective of personal relationships. If you are a woman in a male-dominated environment, there are risks associated with being perceived as over-friendly and of having your behaviour being misconstrued.

There may be times where it is expected for a woman to be more likeable, more accommodating and to fit an outdated stereotype than would not be expected of a man in the same environment. It could be that in the attempt to obtain a level of likeability and to fit into the office dynamic, women feel as though they need to suppress their opinions, needs or ideas. Dampening down and diminishing who they are and what they value to avoid being seen as unapproachable, difficult, over-opinionated or arrogant.

The same is true for what you wear to the office/workplace. While I am sure there are things that men have to consider with regards to their office apparel, I cannot speak to that. I can speak about the thought process for what to wear to work as a woman, especially in a male-dominated environment, which includes questions such as:

- Is this skirt too short? Or too long?
- Is this top too low cut and showing too much cleavage?

- Is what I am wearing too 'girly'?
- Is what I am wearing too masculine?
- Will these shoes make me too tall and result in intimidating others?
- Will I be made fun of for dressing like a wallflower or too much of something (too muted, too little colour, too much colour, etc.)?
- Am I showing too many curves?
- Does this look too sexy?
- Does having my hair up this way make me look like a school ma'am?

And those are just the things that immediately spring to mind! There are more questions, and, needless to say, it is exhausting to worry about these things and what others might think or interpret based on these choices.

When you then bring in the general beauty standards to be a particular size or look a particular way, this adds significant pressure on women in the workplace. This pressure to conform may result in women not dressing and appearing in a manner that is a true representation of their personality and self.

Shortly, we are going to walk through finding the balance between professionalism and femininity. There are situations that for a woman would result in being seen as irrational, over-emotional, bossy or a bitch, whereas the same labels would not be attributed to men in those same situations. Sadly, I could fill this book with examples from my own experience.

What I am about to share with you are the tip of the iceberg. These are things that have been said to me at various times throughout my career:

- "Look at how she's laughing with the men in her team, she must have slept with at least half of them."
- "Oh, here she is, blonde bimbo."
- "How can you come back to work full-time and leave your children at a nursery? What kind of mother are you?"
- "Wow, that's an outfit. Are you on the pull?"
- "You're only agreeing with him because you fancy him."
- "Those shoes [red high heels] aren't work appropriate for someone in leadership."
- [About the same shoes] "Red shoes, no kickers."
- "Can you fix it as well as the boys?"
- "You're so cold. We'll call you the Ice Queen."

When I was younger, knowing how to respond and the fear of my natural response being taken poorly and being judged was very real.

### *Under-representation and perceptions of leadership*

Historically in the technology world, there has been massive under-representation of women in leadership roles and although the gap between men and women in these roles is reducing, typically you will see men in chief information officer (CIO) or chief technology officer (CTO) roles. In fact, when you look at roles such as head of IT, technical architect, infrastructure team leader, these are predominately positions held by men. According to Grant Thornton's 2024 Women in Business data,[8] women hold 32% of senior management positions in the tech sector and only 20.2% of CTO positions in mid-market technology firms.

**Senior leadership positions women hold in the tech industry**

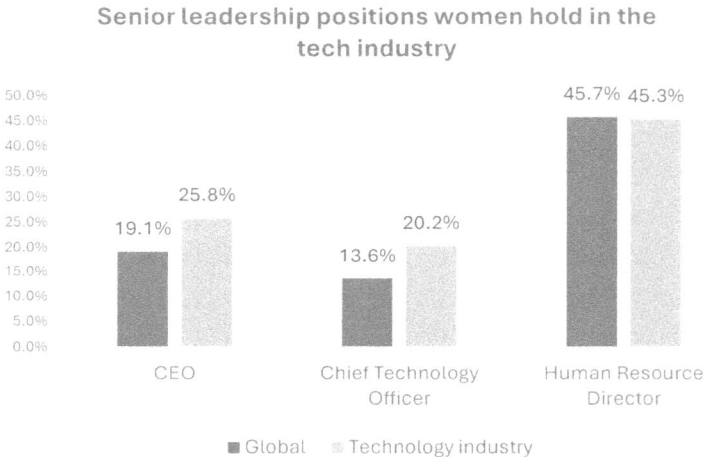

Figure 1: Senior Leadership Positions Women Hold in the Tech Industry

*Source: Grant Thornton's International Business Report (IBR), author's version of the graph*

The graph above from the same Grant Thornton research in 2024 perfectly illustrates the point of under-representation of women in leadership roles, particularly in the technology industry. What does this mean? Well, for the excited young woman starting a career in tech and looking for identifiable

---

[8] *https://www.grantthornton.global/en/insights/women-in-business/women-in-tech-a-pathway-to-gender-balance-in-top-tech-roles/.*

role models, they may not find ones of the same gender to relate to, creating an instant barrier in their career, being unable to see a way of breaking through the glass ceiling to attain a leadership position.

Then there are the behaviours of those in leadership positions and the question: "Would a woman feel as though she needed to conform to adopt the approaches and behaviours of a man in the same position?" If she would, would that be a style and approach that reflects her personal values and individuality? There are more questions here, but following on from the previous barrier discussion, what does this mean in terms of judgement and the pressure to conform?

We have already spoken about the perception of women in the workplace and some of the societal and stereotypical views in a general sense, but what about perceptions of women in the workplace in leadership positions? Are there concerns or barriers about a woman's leadership style, approach, position, etc.? What about if she has children? Does this mean she will not be fully focused? What about if she does not have children? Does this mean she is cold, selfish and a dragon? Obviously (or I hope obviously), we know the answers to these questions are not relevant and whether someone has children or not is completely unrelated to their ability to lead. However, these are things that women will consider as they progress through their career and, sadly for some, these barriers and thought processes will impact their ability to be true to themselves and to represent their authentic self when at work.

### *Workplace inequality*

Diving straight into this topic, we will start with one of the most recognised inequalities between the genders in the workplace: money.

The gender pay gap is real. Women are often paid less than men filling the same or similar roles.

Here are details about the gender pay gap taken from the 2024 report compiled by the Office for National Statistics in the UK[9]:

- *"The gender pay gap has been declining slowly over time; over the last decade it has fallen by approximately a quarter among full-time employees, and in April 2024, it stood at 7.0%, down from 7.5% in 2023.*
- *The gender pay gap is larger for employees aged 40 years and over than those aged under 40 years.*
- *The gender pay gap is larger among high earners than among lower-paid employees.*
- *In April 2024, the gender pay gap was highest in skilled trades occupations and lowest in the caring, leisure and other service occupations.*
- *In April 2024, the gender pay gap among full-time employees was higher in every English region than in Wales, Scotland, or Northern Ireland.*
- *The gender pay gap measures the difference between average hourly earnings excluding overtime of men and*

---

[9] *https://www.ons.gov.uk/employmentandlabourmarket/peopleinwork/earningsandworkinghours/bulletins/genderpaygapintheuk/2024.*

*women, as a proportion of men's average hourly earnings excluding overtime; it is a measure across all jobs in the UK, not of the difference in pay between men and women for doing the same job."*

The survey is the compilation of all gender-pay-gap reports submitted or created by organisations in the United Kingdom. It is an average. Although it is encouraging that the gender pay gap is reducing over time, there is the issue that it exists at all. And when you consider the points about age, high earners and skilled occupations, this is particularly disappointing.

A woman working in a role aiming for promotion, competing against her male peers, may be less inclined to be truly authentic to avoid damaging her opportunities – especially when you consider this barrier with some of the others we have already mentioned such as the pressure to conform and succeed.

Workplace inequality stretches beyond the difference in how much women are paid compared to men. I must highlight here that when I am talking about my experience in the workplace, it is from the perspective of a white woman in the UK. I am aware of further inequalities for women of colour and of other nationalities. In the March 2025 article "Women in tech statistics: The hard truths of an uphill battle" from CIO.com,[10] they state:

*"Women of color face more significant challenges in the tech industry. While a total of 27% of computing roles are*

---

[10] *https://www.cio.com/article/201905/women-in-tech-statistics-the-hard-truths-of-an-uphill-battle.html.*

*held by women, only 3% and 2% are held by Black and Hispanic women, respectively, according to Accenture. Out of 390 women of color in tech surveyed, only 8% said it's easy for them to thrive, compared to 21% of all women. In less-inclusive company cultures, 62% of women of color say they've experienced inappropriate remarks or comments, a number that drops to 14% for inclusive cultures."*

The article continues to talk about the barriers to promotion that women face, citing data from a 2022 McKinsey report[11] that found *"that only 87 women and 82 women of color are promoted to manager for every 100 men across every industry, but when isolated for tech, that number drops to 52 women for every 100 men."*[12]

As a white woman, I will never be able to fully understand the additional barriers faced by women of colour, nor any additional challenges they face. This also applies to other minorities who are marginalised. It is important for me to pause here and acknowledge that my experiences as a white woman are limited to this perspective. I hope that this book is written in a way that will support everyone who wants to embrace their full authenticity, regardless of their race, ethnicity, nationality, gender, sexual preference, or any other minority group.

Starting with recognition, some women feel pressure to mute themselves when it comes to celebrating their achievements,

---

[11] *https://wiw-report.s3.amazonaws.com/Women_in_the_Workplace_2022.pdf.*

[12] Wording taken from CIO.com article in footnote 10.

or find it harder for their work to be recognised, which can lead to a level of masking that does not reflect who they genuinely are. There are certainly examples from throughout my career where I have seen back-slapping and praise for the men in equivalent roles to me for completing tasks that are part and parcel of the role, and yet when completing those same tasks, there was little or no recognition for me. It was expected that I would complete such things without any praise or acknowledgement. I can attest to the fact that this is frustrating and can lead to a reflection on whether personal behaviours and approaches need to change.

Speaking of expectations, as the female in the room, I have been expected at times to keep the meeting minutes or do the associated admin tasks, and the men have not. Many women have told me that they have been the most senior person in the room yet newcomers have assumed that the woman there is an executive assistant or in a supporting role, so have asked them to fetch them a cup of tea or coffee. This links back into the whole patriarchal demarcation between pink and blue tasks and jobs, where societal conditioning results in double standards, or unfair and unequal expectations.

### Imposter syndrome

This is not something that is unique to women as imposter syndrome can raise its ugly head at any time for anyone, however, this can differ between men and women in the workplace. The Harvard Business School published an article in February 2024[13] that discusses how women are less likely to apply for a role if they do not meet all the

---

[13] https://www.library.hbs.edu/working-knowledge/breaking-through-the-self-doubt-that-keeps-talented-women-from-leading.

requirements, whereas men will apply when they meet only 60% of the requirements or qualifications needed for the role. Thinking about this logically, the cause is not purely imposter syndrome as there will be other factors at play, but imposter syndrome is likely to be taking centre stage and stepping up for its monologue.

The 2020 KPMG Women's Leadership Summit Report[14] found that *"as many as 75 percent of executive women report having personally experienced Imposter Syndrome at certain points in their career"*. The study also discovered that 56% *"have been afraid the people around them will not believe they are as capable as expected"*.

### *Limited support networks*

If you google "women in business support network", it will bring back c900,000,000 search results. This would give you the impression that finding and accessing a support network should not be a barrier to being authentic in the workplace as a woman. But when you are starting your career and opening yourself to the working world, you are typically focused on the sphere in which you are working – you may not even consider googling support networks or that being part of one may be useful. You may have some connections outside of the organisation where you work, but it may be that the company you work for has no dedicated support network or groups that provide support for women.

You may not even realise that support networks are something you would find useful and a resource from which to obtain guidance, advice and somewhere to meet like-

---

[14] *https://assets.kpmg.com/content/dam/kpmg/sk/pdf/2020/2020-KPMG-Womens-Leadership-Summit-Report.pdf.*

minded people. Certainly, when I was starting out in my first full-time role 25 years ago, I would not have had the confidence or courage to 'network', and I did not even think of trying to get involved in something outside of work. I was far too busy and preoccupied with just getting through the everyday, and figuring out the basics of being an adult that the education system does not prepare you for.

## Sexual harassment and discrimination

Sexual harassment in the workplace exists. Unfortunately, sexist, misogynistic, derogatory and discriminatory comments are made on a daily basis.

It would be great to say that we have made leaps and bounds to reduce the frequency of these things happening, but after nearly 24 years of working in technology, it saddens me to say that it appears to be a slow burner, and we must keep plugging away to address poor behaviours and holding people to account.

Speaking from experience, this is a very real barrier to authenticity that takes some practice and skill to combat. During my career (so far), I have had to deal with the below and I assure you, this is not the full list but illustrates my point:

- A stalker;
- Multiple unwanted advances;
- Rumours and gossiping;
- Unfounded accusations that I have been promoted because of my gender or implying inappropriate workplace relationships; and
- Bullying and harassment because of my gender.

Imagine having a boss who behaves inappropriately towards you at work and having to try to manage that situation and be your authentic self. Even with the best support networks in the world, it is likely to feel isolating and scary.

If you have the opportunity to read *Allyship Actually*[15] by Lucy Grimwade and David Barrow, I strongly recommend you do so. The book is made up of multiple real-world examples of sexual harassment and discrimination, and the importance of allies in the workplace. Reading the accounts of events that have happened to multiple characters (real people!) is both shocking and incredibly saddening.

### *Emotional labour*

There are occasions in the workplace where women are expected to undertake activities that have the potential to be considered emotional labour, such as mediating conflicts, providing emotional support for colleagues and driving a positive working environment. This does not mean that men are not expected to do these things, but there is often additional pressure for women because of being seen as a 'motherly' or 'big sisterly' figure in the workplace.

What if you do not want to do those pieces of work that are expected of you as a woman? What if it is not in your remit but your manager is asking you to do it? What if you work somewhere where being your authentic self is difficult when you face these types of expectations? How are you supposed to manage pushing back and being authentically you without

---

[15] *Allyship Actually – Why it's 'We' and not 'Me'* by Lucy Grimwade and David Barrow. Available at: https://www.itgovernance.co.uk/shop/product/allyship-actually-why-its-we-and-not-me?.

overstepping the mark or calling out the behaviour in a way that is professional?

Interestingly, before starting writing this book, this was an area that I had not considered until I began my research into being authentic and the barriers that exist. Upon reflection, post research, it is surprising that this barrier had not occurred to me before as throughout my career I have been called 'maternal' or the equivalent in the office, as well as some male colleagues using me as a sounding board for a variety of personal problems despite not being a counsellor!

### Balancing professionalism and femininity

There are many books on this topic. There are jokes made in many television programmes and in comedy sketches. One example that springs to mind is a skit with Olivia Colman, where she is speaking to a woman who has designed a computer for women[16] – a computer that has larger keys to allow for long fingernails, that has the space bar as an emery board (nail file), a tissue dispenser and a vanity mirror. It is funny to watch but at the same time, it highlights some of those stereotypes that make the balance between being professional and being feminine challenging.

Slightly different but also closely related is the issue of perceived masculine traits in men. I would say there are significant (and maybe larger) workplace problems with 'masculine' traits and what is and is not considered professional – perhaps most abruptly seen in blue-collar (traditionally very male) industries and roles. Think building trades, manufacturing, armed forces. The need to be seen as

---

[16] *https://www.youtube.com/watch?v=iVquI-MVmd0*.

'masculine' in these types of industries and roles, and thereby 'accepted', is a huge barrier to authenticity for men.

Going back to something mentioned earlier, there is the question of what professionalism looks like and how that ideal differs from person to person. It is possible that professionalism, and the perception of what constitutes being professional, will also differ based on the industry or sector. From my perspective, this is particularly true of working in male-dominated environments, such as technology. The characteristics of a typical professional working in technology are likely to include being logic-based, highly technical, introverted, socially awkward and someone who discusses complex ideas and solutions in a binary manner. The technology sector can be seen as a cold, hard environment that has no space for being empathetic, people-focused or with any display of emotion (for reference, see any episode of Channel 4's *The IT Crowd*,[17] which features Richmond, who lives in the basement).

The ideal of femininity does not align with that view of a person working in technology. Women are seen (and portrayed) as highly emotional, illogical, warm, soft, etc., with the expectation that they can host a party without any social anxiety, they can engage with anyone in small talk without the slightest thought. For a woman working in technology, there are decades worth of stigma and stereotypes to break through, which can feel like too big a hurdle to jump when it comes to being authentic in the workplace.

---

[17] *https://www.channel4.com/programmes/the-it-crowd.*

## 3: Barriers for women in the workplace

There is a double standard associated with balancing professionalism and femininity. Table 1 shows professional statements alongside reactions to them based on whether the person making the statement is a woman or a man. What do you think about the categorisation of the reactions to a female speaker versus to a male speaker? Do you think these words are correct descriptors or that they are based on gender stereotypes or bias?

**Table 1: Double Standards**

| Professional statement | Reaction to a woman | | Reaction to a man |
|---|---|---|---|
| "Your document needs more work" | Abrasive | | Helpful |
| "We should rethink this and take a different approach" | Disruptive | | Pragmatic disruptor |
| "This is frustrating" | Emotional | vs. | Passionate |
| "I am the best person to deliver this project for you" | Arrogant | | Confident |
| "I'm in the middle of something; can | Bitch | | Focused |

| we catch up later?" | | | |
|---|---|---|---|
| "I need that report by the end of the day" | Bossy | | Time-focused |

All these barriers or challenges can be addressed or managed to allow you to find that sweet balance between being professional and being feminine, if you choose to do so. More on that later.

**We asked, you spoke – survey time**

While preparing this book, it was important to obtain data from outside my own thoughts and perceptions. So, using the power of LinkedIn, I posted four polls in October 2024 asking my network the following questions:

1. Do you feel you can be your authentic self at work?
2. What are the barriers to authenticity?
3. Is it easier for men to be authentic in the workplace?
4. Is there an industry where being authentic is harder?

As is the way with social media, the reach of these polls was subject to the algorithm and the logic behind it. There is information that is not easily available such as response by gender, age bracket, role level, etc., unless you scroll through the respondents and check out their LinkedIn profiles. The average response was 62 individuals and the estimated split between the sexes was 57% of respondents as male and 43% as female, using a basic calculation.

I also shared an anonymous survey asking more in-depth questions to understand more detail of what the general consensus was with regard to being authentic at work. The survey also asked for demographic information, although these were not mandatory questions. The survey had fewer responses than the LinkedIn polls, with a total of 24 respondents, where the gender split was 33% women, 50% men and 17% opted to not share their gender.

Here is a look into the data and we will do a side-by-side comparison where applicable to show any difference in results.

## Do you feel as though you can be your authentic self at work?

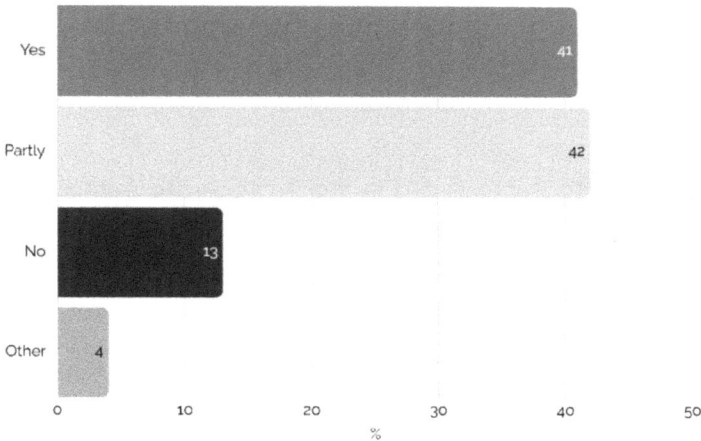

**Figure 2: Do You Feel as Though You Can Be Your Authentic Self at Work: LinkedIn Survey Results**

# Do you feel as though you can be your authentic self at work?

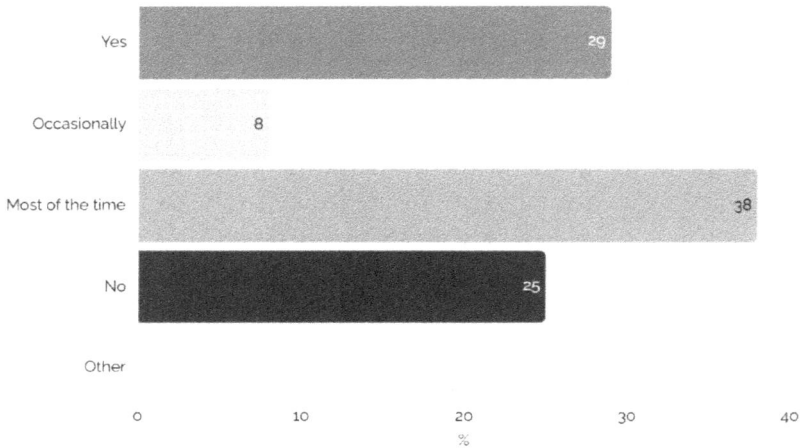

**Figure 3: Do You Feel as Though You Can Be Your Authentic Self at Work: In-depth Survey Results**

# What are the barriers to authenticity?

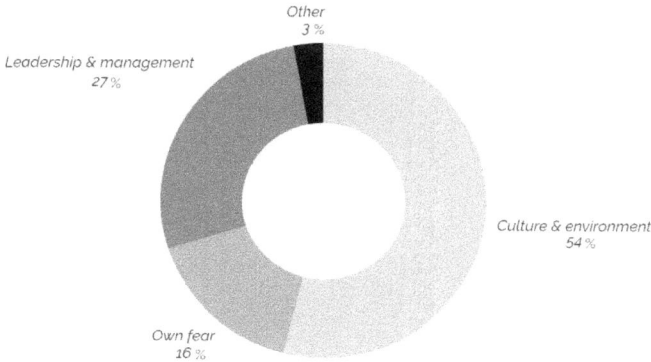

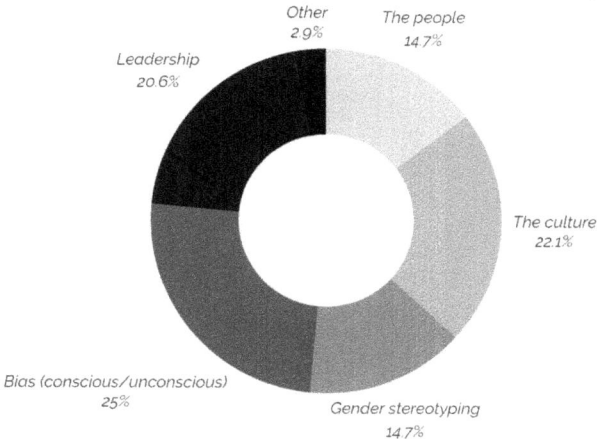

Other
3 %

Leadership & management
27 %

Culture & environment
54 %

Own fear
16 %

**Figure 4: What are the Barriers to Authenticity? LinkedIn Results**

# What are the barriers to authenticity?

Other
2.9%

The people
14.7%

Leadership
20.6%

The culture
22.1%

Bias (conscious/unconscious)
25%

Gender stereotyping
14.7%

**Figure 5: What are the Barriers to Authenticity? In-depth Survey Results**

## Is it easier for men to be authentic in the workplace?

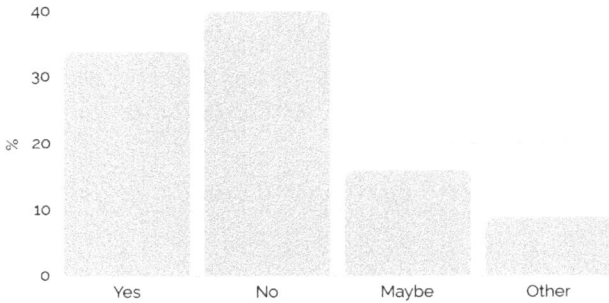

**Figure 6: Is It Easier for Men to Be Authentic in the Workplace? LinkedIn Results**

## Is there a difference between the genders when it comes to being authentic at work?

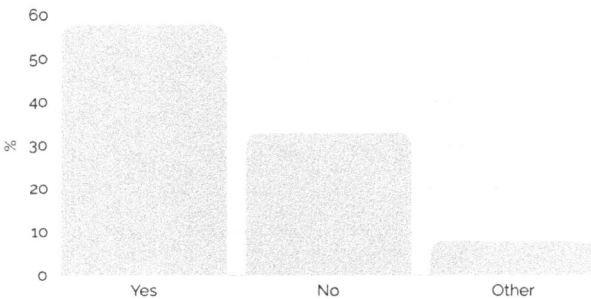

**Figure 7: Is There a Difference Between the Genders When it Comes to Being Authentic at Work? In-depth Survey Results**

While there are some differences in the results, there are key data points to call out:

- Less than 50% of all respondents from both the polls and the survey felt that they could be their authentic self in the workplace.
- From the anonymous survey, 58% of respondents (62 individuals in total) believed that there is a difference between the genders when it comes to being authentic.
- Both polls and the survey had correlating responses to the barriers to authenticity:
  o Culture and environment;
  o Own fear (shown in the results from LinkedIn polls);
  o Leadership; and
  o Gender stereotyping and bias (conscious and unconscious).

The final question on the anonymous survey was: "Is there anything you'd like to add about being authentic at work, the barriers, challenges or positives associated with it?" Here are some of the answers:

*"When you can be yourself, you are comfortable in your skin and feel trusted to get on with the job, when you can't be yourself or people around you aren't their authentic self, then there's always a sense of people holding back and you can['t] truly gel."*

*"I have learnt over the years that I am more at ease, comfortable, happier and productive etc by just being me! Took me years to get to this space and once there it's a win*

*all round – everyone benefits. A much happier personal and work life."*

*"It's hard to know if males and females feel the same."*

*"I think the primary challenge comes with ensuring that your 'authentic self' still remains professional. It's easy to overstep the mark or for the lines to be become blurred – Neither is ideal."*

*"I get more done with less effort when I can be myself. I can get a LOT done when I have to hide who I am, but eventually this makes me depressed and starts a self-harm cycle."*

*"I think not being able to be authentic in the workplace just puts some natural blockers, personality-wise. Hence, if I block what is natural to me, how can I be my best self professionally?"*

*"Sometimes the values of a company are not reality day to day."*

*"Social stigma. As a neurodivergent, it took me decades to 'come out' as ND at work."*

*"Masking is becoming the norm. Whether it is hiding insecurities or acting 'upwards' in our roles to try and be seen or get a promotion. However, I believe people actually care less about work [post] COVID and see it as just a means to an end. The career high life isn't important anymore. Having enough counts for more."*

*"Leaders pretending to be authentic and selling themselves on that brand whilst stymying or reprimanding others for actually being authentic."*

*"You can have a mask for work that has an extrovert image, when normally you might be an introvert."*

What you get from these responses is an insight into the barriers the individuals have faced, such as social conditioning, limited support networks, imposter syndrome, fear of rejection, toxic leadership and environments, etc.

## So many barriers

The topic of what 'authenticity' is and what stops someone from being authentic could be discussed at much greater length, with many studies and psychologists weighing in on the subject to provide their expertise. From what you have read here, you should now have a good picture of what it means to be authentic and the variety of barriers for all the sexes and some of the specific barriers that women experience in this space.

Now it is time to move on to how to break this down for yourself, how you can drive yourself to a positive mindset where being authentic at work is second nature, and how you can do this without thinking, like second nature and in a way that balances who you are as an individual while maintaining the appropriate level of professionalism.

# CHAPTER 4: WHAT ARE YOUR VALUES?

> Your values make up who we are and what matters to you, and underpin your beliefs. Your values are the cornerstones of your authenticity.

In this chapter, we are going to be talking about knowing yourself and how knowing what you value is one of the foundations to being authentic. It is time for us to talk about values, understanding more about where they come from. As well as talking about how to define your values and what that process looks like.

Values are individual and unique to each person in the same way as their fingerprints are unique. You may have values in common with other people, but the reason why you value these things will be based on a variety of experiences and upbringing that still makes them unique to you.

Understanding where values come from is more complex than you would think. The make-up of someone's belief system stems from such a range of sources that we need to go back to the beginning. The beginning being that a set of values was introduced to you as a child from your family, your upbringing, the beliefs of the adults around you, through stories and through your social networks.

Let us go back in time to your childhood…

To understand your values as an adult, it is important to spend time thinking about where they come from. Children learn a core set of values through:

- Their parents and family;

- Teachers and the school environment; and
- Their friends.

They also learn values through other sources, such as:

- Television;
- Films;
- Social media;
- Public figures; and
- Books.

Before we get deeper into this, let me be perfectly clear. Although I have an interest in psychology and what makes people tick, I am not an expert in this field. I have invested time, thought and research into the topic of values, but what I am about to discuss is my personal opinion. If you want to know more about the psychology behind where values come from, I would suggest doing your own research.

If you think back to your parents and teachers when you were growing up, it is unlikely they will have said: "Now then, today I'm going to tell you what your values are." Children are typically taught values through rules, cautionary tales and stories which may have their origins in a particular faith, or family/societal background. For example, the below are typical rules given to children:

- Do not tell lies.
- Play nicely.
- Be kind to your friends.
- Share with others.
- Do not be rude.
- Do what you are told.

- Respect your elders.
- Work hard.
- Always try your best.
- Do not be afraid to try things.

If you consider these rules through a different lens, they all have a basis in a defined value:

**Table 2: Rules and Values**

| Rule | Value |
|------|-------|
| Do not tell lies | Honesty, integrity |
| Play nicely | Being considerate, teamwork |
| Be kind to your friends | Compassion, empathy |
| Share with others | Cooperation, collaboration |
| Do not be rude | Honesty*, respect, kindness, compassion |
| Do what you are told | Integrity, being ethical, moralistic, dutiful |
| Respect your elders | Respect, compassion, being dutiful |
| Work hard | Conscientiousness, dedication, passion |

| Always try your best | Passion, inspiration, resilience |
| Do not be afraid to try things | Courage, determination |

* It's fair to say that sometimes to not be rude may require a "white lie" and being slightly dishonest. For example, if you're asked, "Does my bum look big in this?" answering with total honesty may upset the person asking the question. Rather than saying, "Yes" you may choose to say a softer version of the truth like, "I don't think that's the most flattering, but if you feel confident then go for it", or something similar.

As an adult, you have the opportunity to define your own values and invest time into understanding what builds the foundations of who you are. I have been a mentor for two decades and in the first session with a new mentee, we discuss the areas they want to work on and develop – it is in these sessions that I open the conversation about values. At the end of the first session, I give my mentee a piece of homework to do at their own pace (with a list of resources that you can find at the end of this book), and that homework is – yes, you have guessed it – to spend time considering and defining their values.

This may sound like a relatively easy piece of homework but figuring out what your foundations are as an adult is quite a challenge. It requires a level of vulnerability to open yourself up to question your beliefs and the building blocks placed by your childhood.

## How to define your values

What may start as a seemingly easy exercise will rapidly become challenging to narrow down your values. It is like when you are doing a big clear-out or spring clean – it starts off well with lots of motivation and a clear vision of what is going to happen. Then you get halfway through and have a pile of 'stuff' in the middle of the room that needs sorting, some of which you will get distracted by and other bits will be a case of trying to figure out if you need them or not. The advice here is to take it in bite-sized chunks. You do not need to get to your values in one sitting. You can split the task up over time to give you the headspace and time to consider the 'what' and 'why'.

But how do you define your values? Here is the process I typically follow and have advised my mentees to follow:

### *Phase one (~ 2 hours)*

1. Find some time where you are not too tired or distracted to focus on the task at hand (so, not after a particularly stressful day at work, or straight after an intense workout, or dealing with a family crisis).
2. Sit somewhere comfortable, where you can stay relaxed and open to possibilities. (I like to sit in my kitchen with a view out to the garden, maybe with the doors open to allow air in and potentially a cheeky glass of Prosecco or a nice cold/hot drink.)
3. If you are 'old school' like me, have a pen and pad of paper ready to make notes, doodle and write thoughts down.

4. You will need access to the Internet, so either a smartphone, tablet or computer.
5. Go to websites like:
   a. Mindtools: What Are Your Values?[18]
   b. Brené Brown: Dare to Lead: List of Values[19]
   c. Better Up: Personal values examples[20]

   and look at the ranges of words available relating to values. At this point in the exercise, it can be a casual skim read to see what words are there and if anything stands out. For example, when I see words like "empathy", "integrity", "honesty" they typically jump out at me in a list.
6. Start writing down any words that really resonate with you. It does not matter how many you write down – what you are doing at the moment is getting a feel for a plethora of words that may end up being culled when you refine them, but for now, do not worry if you write down lots of words.

---

[18] *https://www.mindtools.com/a5eygum/what-are-your-values.*

[19] *https://brenebrown.com/resources/dare-to-lead-list-of-values/.*

[20] *https://www.betterup.com/blog/personal-values-examples.*

7. The sweet spot for the number of values you are heading towards is between five and seven,[21] but you are unlikely to get to that number on your first pass. This is OK and it is probably that during this phase you will have a list of up to 20-30 words at first.

8. When you have finished writing down all the words that resonate with you, pause and take a moment. Are you still in the right frame of mind to continue with defining your values, or do you need time to go away, reflect and come back for the next step? Either option is fine – these are your values and there is no definitive or 'right' way to do this.

> **Tip:**
> Utilise the resources available on the internet, in books or even using generative AI to support this first phase of defining your values.

### Phase two (~1 hour)

9. When you are ready, it is time to look at the list and start sifting through the words you have written down. There

---

[21] The goal is five to seven. Fewer than five does not typically give you a fully rounded perspective of what makes you tick and builds the foundations (the cornerstones) of your authenticity. Any more than seven is a lot and when you are doing any reflection on whether situations, people, organisations, etc. align with your values, you will need to consider all 25 (or whatever number you go for). You want your values to work for you, not make it harder for you.

are lots of ways to do this, but here are a few suggestions:

a. Get some highlighter pens or different colours and start highlighting the words on a scale of the following:

    i. Yes, definitely something I value.

    ii. Yeah, I do value this but there are other words that resonate more.

    iii. Maybe, but probably not.

    iv. No, this is not one of my values (it may be something others value, but it does not make my first cut).

b. Circle the words you absolutely resonate with and cross out the words you do not.

c. Working from the list, create a second list of words using a process of elimination to refine it (this could be through selecting one word that encapsulates others, or through a straight prioritisation call).

10. Again, take a moment to pause and reflect on whether you are happy to continue or whether you need to come back to it. If you are carrying on, make sure you take a brief break to stretch your legs, get a fresh drink and settle back into the next phase.

## *Phase three (~ 2 hours)*

11. OK, time to go to the next round of refining the list of words to get to your values. Start with looking at the values that are a 'maybe' or 'yeah, but I resonate with other words more'.

12. Go through the words and ask yourself these questions:
    a. Do I value this?
        i. If yes, why? Does it replace any words already in the 'yes' bucket?
        ii. If no, discard it from the list.
    b. Is the word similar to other words in the list?
        i. If yes, does this word work as a better descriptor for the others? If the answer to this is no, then discard it from the list.
        ii. If no, what is it about this word that resonates with you? Again, ask whether it replaces any words already in the list.

    Your aim here is to remove any of the 'maybe' words so you have got one solid list of values that you will then need to refine.

13. At this point, after having done this second round of refining the list, I would create a third list of words. This is partly because I do not like seeing things crossed out, but also it will be useful to see your journey to getting to your values and the process you have taken to get there.

14. You should now have one single list of 'yes' words that you need to refine. And again, this is time to reflect, pause and ensure you are ready for the final phase of defining your values. The next phase is going to be the toughest, so make sure you are ready, present and can dedicate the time for phase four.

### *Phase four (~2–3 hours)*

15. Now it is time to get your five to seven keywords that are your values. Depending on the number of words you have left on your sheet, this may take a longer time than each of the previous phases. It is OK to break this into bite-sized chunks.

16. Looking at the words on your list, are there any logical groupings that you can put them together in to help refine them? For example, words like 'honesty', 'trustworthiness', 'openness' and 'transparency' could be grouped together as they are all similar and are often used when describing each other. If there are not any obvious logical groupings, just skip to the next step.

17. Look at each word in turn and spend some time thinking about what it is about that word that resonates with you. Assess them critically and objectively to continue the process of elimination. If the word still resonates, keep it, but if it does not or the rationale for having it on the list is not as compelling as others, discard it.

18. Keep going round this loop until you get to your goal of five to seven words that are your values.

19. Once you have narrowed down your selection, get out another piece of paper/note on your phone or computer and jot down your newly defined values.

And, of course, give yourself a pat on the back for completing the task. I suspect it will have been insightful, potentially confronting at times, but the journey to get there is worthwhile!

**Tip:**

**Your goal is to have between 5 and 7 values.**

## I have got my values, now what?

It is worth taking a moment to acknowledge that you have just achieved defining the core of what makes you, your personality and belief system. Now that you have a written list of what is important to you and why, under the heading of 'key values', you can start (or continue) on your path to being authentically you in the workplace (and at home if you are not already).

"How do I do this?", you might ask. "What do I do next?"

### *The cornerstones of your authenticity*

The most important outcome from defining your values is that you have identified the foundations you are working from. You could call them the cornerstones of your authenticity. Understanding your beliefs and what is important to you allows you to do the following:

- Find your way, your direction and achieve clarity – potentially resulting in making decisions more easily through the understanding of what matters to you, what drives you and what makes you who you are.
- Build stronger boundaries – knowing your values means you learn what is acceptable to you and what is not, and builds your ability to say "no" to those things that do not align or push you beyond your comfort zone.
- Build better, stronger relationships – you may attract people with similar values or those who respect yours, achieving a deeper connection and understanding of

others, even those who have different values from your own.

- Align your goals and increase your motivation – you are likely to identify what your goals are more easily and then find more drive to work towards and achieve them.
- Find a sense of peace and acceptance of who you really are – reducing any second-guessing and any internal conflict through understanding your choices and how they reflect who you are.
- Increasing your authenticity – you have learned what makes you tick, what drives you, what matters to you, and learning this will allow you to continue on the journey to authenticity, living and breathing these values. Becoming more fulfilled and comfortable in your own skin, allowing the mask to drop.

It is also worth noting that masking is commonplace in many aspects of your life and there are occasions where characteristics of the mask become part of who you are, they're no longer the shield to hide behind but become part of your skin. Let me explain this using an example: In my line of work, I spend much of my time engaging with colleagues throughout an organisation, across all levels of seniority. I am naturally shy but in a work environment my role needs me to be the opposite so that I can engage effectively with people. What was once a protective mask showing a confidence I did not feel has evolved overtime to become part of who I am in the workplace. It's no longer a mask, the confidence is real and the shyness at work is a thing of the past.

### *Values aren't just for people, they're for organisations too*

Most organisations you work for will have their company values listed on their website, in their performance review (annual appraisal) paperwork that their employees are measured against as well as in their organisational and personal objectives. You now have the ability to see how your values align with those of your employer and spot any gaps. You can also look at any significant differences that may exist and how you feel about any divergence from your beliefs. If your values are vastly different with no alignment at all, what does this make you feel and, importantly, do you need to do anything about it?

The same applies for prospective employers. Remember that when you are being interviewed, it is a two-way street: you are checking out whether it is the right company for you as much as the company is working to understand if you are right for the role. When you are doing your research to learn about the company and what it does (to answer the "tell us what you know about what we do"), also check out the company values. What you are looking to learn is whether from a beliefs perspective this potential new company is aligned with your views of the world, as well as the values the managers expect their employees to live up to. Does the potential employer operate in an industry sector that does not align with your values, e.g. gambling, alcohol, tobacco, defence industries, etc.?

Regardless of whether you are doing the analysis of values for your current company or a prospective one, it is important to note that it is unlikely that your values will wholly align, and this is OK. Why? Because in the same way that you will not have the same interests as all your friends, the differences in values can be an interesting and rewarding learning experience. It could also be a total disaster, but with a positive mindset and reframing the "what if", it could go very well. In essence, what you are doing here is building knowledge so that you can make an informed decision when it comes to companies and your value alignment.

### *Teamwork makes the dream work*

You have done the analysis for the organisation, now what about your team, your peers, your senior leaders, your direct line manager, etc.? When you are engaging with the people that you work with, what do you think their values are? Where do they converge or diverge? What does that mean if they do? How will that impact your relationships? Or even, will it impact your relationships with your colleagues?

Regardless of the role you hold or your position in a business, it is likely that you will need to engage with other humans and, as such, you will need stakeholder-management skills. In my opinion, this is one of the most important skills in the workplace to hone, develop, maintain and grow. And to work with other humans, it is useful to understand what makes them tick – what their values are – because this can help inform you of how best to interact with them. This may sound like there is more to this topic and you are right, but we will discuss this in chapter 6 – "Breaking out the influencing guns".

You can, of course, ask your colleagues what their values are and strike up a conversation about values in general, as it is an interesting topic. You may not have the opportunity to have the same in-depth conversation with your customers or colleagues from the wider business. You may need to observe their behaviour in pressured situations, how they respond to see if you can understand what makes them tick.

For example, if you have an internal stakeholder who is very matter of fact, does not like delayed communication and is focused on key deliverables, it is possible that some of their values may include 'communication', 'transparency', 'timeliness', 'diligence', 'competence', and 'productivity'. Knowing this sort of information is useful.

## It is not once and done – values evolve over time

It is important to note that you cannot just define your values once and it is done. As you learn and grow as an adult, experiencing a variety of situations, outcomes and individuals, your values are likely to change over time.

Your boundaries, and where you are prepared to be flexible and compromise, will change over time along with your values. There are memes about people over a certain age no longer caring about how they are perceived and having a lower tolerance level for poor behaviours – this is because their values will have changed over time. Perhaps they are no longer focusing on the need to find belonging from a wider network and rather focusing on a more select group of individuals with whom they have a deeper connection.

The cornerstones of your values and how this impacts your authenticity will evolve and, as such, you need to revisit the exercise to define, or rather, redefine your values. This is not something you will need to do monthly, or even annually, but it is wise to reconnect with your values on a regular basis (the timing being of your own choosing). It is important to spend time performing some self-reflection periodically to understand if anything has changed in terms of what you value. It can be as often as every other year or every five to ten years; it is all dependent on how YOU want to approach it.

My advice at first would be to check in every couple of years to see if anything has changed significantly and then over time, you will learn the cadence at which you need to spend time reviewing your values. It is important to note that in many respects, it is a much quicker process than defining them in the beginning.

You already have your list of words. It is a case of looking at them with a list of other values nearby and asking the question: "Do I still value the same things or are there other values in the wider list that resonate with me more?" Then going back through the process of elimination in phases three and four to refine those values and update your list.

> **Tip:**
> Whilst it can be useful to gain insight from others when defining your values, remember they are a deeply personal thing. What a value means to you, may mean something different to someone else.

**Sharing my values**

Part of being my authentic self is being open about who I am and not being afraid to share information about myself. I have always been someone who openly talks about emotions, feelings and various aspects of my life. Of course, there are some things that are private, but in the general sense, I am happy to be an open book.

In that vein, here are my values, with an explanation of why they are important to me. I will also provide some context of how my values have changed over time. The reason for sharing this is to provide you with some context of why I consider them important to me, so that when you are going through your own values definition, perhaps it will strike a chord with you. Some of these may resonate with you and other parts not so much, but as we walk through my values and how they are the foundations of who I am professionally and personally, I hope it will provide inspiration or insight to support you on your journey.

These are my values from the high level:

- Authenticity
- Family (not in the typical sense)
- Honesty
- Empathy
- Integrity
- Courage
- Independence

Before breaking them down to give you context, it is important to share with you that these values have evolved over time as I have aged and grown as an individual. There are four core values that have been there from the beginning, which are **authenticity, honesty, family** and **empathy**. These have been a constant, but when I last reviewed my values, I realised that there were other areas that are important to me and so my list expanded to seven core values.

### *Authenticity*

This may seem like an obvious choice of a value and perhaps it is, but for me, authenticity is important. Not just from myself but from the people around me. I have a kind of superpower where I can see more of what is going on with the people around me than perhaps they are meaning to portray. This could be considered a type of empathy but it is more than the recognition of another person's feelings as it includes a sense of whether that person is being sincere. If you imagine a barometer for humans, whether they are genuine or less so, I am quite good at gauging at lot about other people.

Although, this superpower is by no means foolproof.

Going back to valuing authenticity – I want to have real conversations and have a real connection with people. Having spent years at school being bullied, as well as experiencing bullying at college, university and in the workplace, I am not interested in subterfuge or in those who hide their true selves for the sake of popularity or who put down or shame others. I respect those people who march to their own beat, who are unapologetic about who they are as an individual, and I tend to be drawn to them, even if our values do not wholly align.

My values have changed as I have experienced more of the world personally and professionally. The more I have engaged with a variety of different people, personality types, leaders and colleagues, I have recognised where my values needed to be added to or changed. For me, having these labels or words to live by helps me maintain my direction, being able to focus my attentions on my ultimate goals as a human and driving my authenticity by living by them.

I am curious about others and even if I do not share the same views or beliefs, I always want people to be comfortable being who they are. There is no need for pretence, and I would like others to be comfortable being themselves around me.

### *Family (not in the typical sense)*

If you have read the "About the author" section, you will know a bit of my background. My family is extended through my stepsiblings and siblings where we share one parent. I did not grow up in the typical family environment and my life has been all the richer because of it. I learned from an early age that family was not necessarily those you are connected to by blood. There are people in my group of friends that I consider as sisters and brothers rather than just friends – our bond is that strong and they mean as much to me as my blood relatives.

In addition to this, I am like the typical 'momma bear' when it comes to my children and stepchild. My sense of loyalty and devotion to my family (in all its guises) is a cornerstone of who I am as a person.

My family goes beyond those that would be on the genetic family tree. In my opinion, being blood-related to someone does not mean you have to love nor like them – it is in the actions and depth of the relationship where you find true kinship, and this is something I value.

### *Honesty*

The truth is not always pretty and sometimes it is downright hard to hear, but I believe it is better to hear the hard truth than to be plied with false platitudes. Unfortunately, you will meet people in the course of your life who are not always truthful, or they are telling you a version of the truth from their point of view. This is most definitely something I have experienced. I have felt the hurt, the mistrust, the disappointment and pain from dishonest behaviours.

When I have encountered dishonest behaviours in the workplace, I often feel frustrated as well as disappointed. Why? Because:

- You can learn from honesty.
- You can trust those who are honest.
- You can admire those who are honest and be inspired by their courage.
- You can identify development areas and opportunities for growth through honesty.

I am a forthright person; however, I like to allow the truth to land softly, always considering the other person and how they receive information. Empathy is at my core, as you will see in my next value.

If someone has feedback or information for me, I want to know the facts and understand the rationale behind it. It helps me understand and gives me a basis to work from.

### *Empathy*

Everything we do in this world will involve interacting with other people. I do not know what it is like to walk in the shoes of the people around me, but it is important for me to try to understand. We are all humans together, whether we like it or not. To understand the emotions of others and get some insight into why they are who they are and how they behave is important to building strong relationships that have longevity.

If you lead a team or are a leader (not to be confused with a manager), you should always lead with empathy. Your fellow humans are vital to the success of what you do and, as such, they should be supported, nurtured and invested in. I have had many male managers who have not been able to empathise with me as a woman but instead sought to find a connection or understanding in other ways that allowed them to empathise with who I am, what challenges I have faced and anything that I was working towards.

I am an introvert, and my social battery runs out relatively quickly in social situations – I get 'peopled out' – but I still seek to understand and empathise with others because without human connection, who are we?

## *Integrity*

Doing what I say I will do, being true to my word and delivering on promises is important to me.

Why?

I have had experiences where my work, my ethics and my authenticity were questioned in the workplace in a way that I have not witnessed happen to my male peers. While I have not necessarily felt discriminated against to any great extent, I have always felt as though I needed to go the extra mile to prove myself and ensure that I act with integrity. I am not perfect by any stretch of the imagination and all humans are fallible, however, I always try to ensure my intentions are pure of heart, and I believe in what I am doing.

For me, integrity is linked to reputation. As a woman in technology, or a woman in business full stop, my reputation is important. I have seen others have their reputations unfairly tarnished because of failing to deliver or meet expectations. I do not want to be that person. I want to be treated fairly, working to the same rules as EVERYONE around me.

My intentions are pure. I am honest. I do what I say I will or set expectations if I am not going to be able to deliver on a promise. And, as such, I greatly respect and value those who act with integrity.

In my experience, those managers who set false expectations or fail to deliver are the ones I have the least faith in and lose respect for. I would not want to be viewed as such myself, and therefore value integrity.

### Courage

In terms of valuing courage, it is not about acts of bravery in the typical sense. Sometimes, courage is standing firm and going against the tide. Sometimes, there is more courage in surviving. There are other times where being courageous is to stand out from the crowd, questioning the status quo, voicing an opinion or stating a fact that will not land favourably with the others in the room.

It takes courage to be your authentic self. Based on my values so far, are you surprised that this is important to me?

### Independence

Lastly and by no means least, I value independence.

This does not mean that I have to fly solo and go it alone. It links closely with courage in that I believe it is important to stand on your own two feet. To not be afraid to follow your own path and strive for what may not be the established norm but is right for you.

I can say, hand on heart, that everything I have achieved so far both professionally and personally is because I have stood for what I believe in and forged my own path. I have not done it completely alone, having sought advice, guidance and support from others, but my path has been my own. I march to my own beat and will continue to do so.

Independence in this sense also means knowing when to ask for help. We are not islands. It is OK to seek help and recognise those times where you need the support of others to help you achieve your goals.

# CHAPTER 5: WHAT ARE YOU AFRAID OF?

> Exploring typical challenges for women in tech and in male-dominated sectors. Understanding what barriers exist today to build a list of action areas to focus on and break down the walls.

"What are you afraid of?" This question can be confronting and scary to answer because whilst the answer is quite often very clear, it can be a daunting thought to actually answer it and prepare to take action.

Being authentic and truly who you are can be incredibly daunting and there is no way of knowing how you will be received by the people around you. One of the barriers to authenticity that we have discussed is the fear of rejection, making you more inclined to conform to what you perceive as the norm. But we are not talking about the generic fear of rejection and the myriad ways to combat that here. No, in this chapter, we are talking about YOUR fear.

What are you specifically afraid of? And how is that manifesting itself in your behaviours?

Back in the beginning of time when humans were literally hunting and gathering along with the other creatures that walked the earth, we developed the 'fight or flight' instinct, which is innately useful in those circumstances where it can literally mean life or death. In today's world, we still have those occasions where it is literally a life-or-death decision and the fight-or-flight instinct kicks in, but should that instinct kick in when it comes to being authentic?

What is going to be interesting as we walk through this topic, is how fear plays into the barriers to being authentic, which we will be discussing further as we progress through this book.

**Start with you**

Before we can address the fear of being yourself in a professional capacity, we need to understand where your fears in general come from. What is it that makes you freeze with fear? What are those things that make you want to run out of a room or situation screaming for your life, not daring to look behind but to keep distancing yourself as much as possible?

I will start by sharing key facts about what scares me to illustrate the point:

- I do not like the dark and, if alone at home at night, I can be seen racing up the stairs on my way to bed as though there is a sea of zombies chasing me in the darkness (yes, I could switch on a light, but I still run because I will have to switch off the light and who knows what lurks in the shadows?!).
- I do not like crowded spaces where the noise is so loud that I cannot hear myself think.
- I do not like confined spaces where I feel small, squashed and as though there is not enough air.
- I do not like social situations where I feel as though everyone else knows each other and I am the newcomer, the interloper and potentially intruding on the relationships of others.

- I do not like being the centre of attention, with all eyes focused on me.
- I do not like having to walk through the door into a pub/bar/restaurant first (in my head, I picture a scene from the movies set in the Wild West when someone walks into a saloon and everyone goes quiet, turning to stare at the person who just walked in).
- I do not like it when I can sense that someone does not like me or is indifferent to me (everyone wants to be liked).
- I do not like heights when it comes to man-made structures but have no issue peering over the edge of a cliff face or a mountainside. (Although I have been crag fast (stuck on a mountainside and unable to move) a number of times because I once fell over on a mountain and hurt myself, so the possibility of falling scares me.)
- I have many reoccurring dreams that have me on a precipice about to fall or in a plane crash or there is a zombie apocalypse.

This list could go on, of course, but that is part of the point I am making. What I have shared above is a list of things that make me uncomfortable or put me outside of my comfort zone or in some cases, have a link to the feeling of not being accepted as a child at school. Most of these 'fears' will have their root in my childhood experiences. Some are linked to adult experiences earlier on in my career that have tried to take hold of me, like a weed, to determine my behaviour or to dampen my authenticity. Of course, there are factors to consider that go beyond the introspective view of my own personality and psyche. The behaviours of others, peer pressure, societal and cultural norms or expectations that can influence behaviour will all have an impact, but let me walk you through some of my fears in more detail. Let us see how they might impact my authenticity.

### The dark

I have always been 'blessed' with an overactive imagination, which has its pluses when it comes to immersing myself in a story. It allows me to embrace a level of creativity that I do not have the skill to express via other channels such as art or music. However, it can also result in overthinking, worry and anxiety that is irrational. All those scary stories we are told as children about the mad axe man wandering down country lanes still have me keeping an eye out for him when driving at night.

From a professional perspective, there are not many times where I have had to face the fear of the dark, but there were times when I was 'on call' (needed to respond to emergency IT incidents out of hours). Occasionally, I was required to go into the office at night to fix a server and then lock the building back up again, ensuring the lights were off. I can tell you for free that the little fire exit signs that glow in the dark have freaked me out on more occasions than I would care to admit. They look ghostly and unnatural.

But how does this fear really link to being authentic? Well, imagine you are in the office and your colleagues are talking about the latest and greatest horror movie and potentially planning a night out to the cinema to watch it. I know that if I go too, every jump scare will see me jumping higher and higher out of my seat, which, while funny, is not necessarily an image I would like my colleagues to have of me. I am not ashamed of being afraid of creepy things but at the same time, is this a part of my persona that I am comfortable sharing with my colleagues? Probably not.

So, I need to find a way to be true to myself and not go to watch something that will keep me awake at night for months. And I need to manage the situation so that I do not portray myself to my colleagues as over-dramatic or having irrational fears. This feeds into the barrier that is the fear of judgement.

### *Crowded or tight spaces*

I am also blessed with tinnitus, which if you do not know already, is a condition where you have a constant ringing or buzzing in your ears. My tinnitus changes from being a quiet hum to being a high-pitched squeal that makes it difficult to concentrate. It is triggered by large, crowded spaces as well as stressful situations like being in a confined space. Sometimes I can ignore it, but at other times it can be very difficult and overwhelming.

This impacts me most when the environment is particularly loud, and I may not catch everything someone is saying the first time. If you add in ambient noise (such as music in a pub, or the general hum of a large crowd or open office), I may not be able to hear anything someone says. I do not have the ability to lip read and I honestly do not know what is socially acceptable when it comes to how many times to ask someone to repeat themselves.

### *Social situations*

I have always been someone who enjoys the company of others but also cherishes the quiet time of my own company. I am an introvert – or probably an ambivert by today's standards – which means that I have a finite amount of energy to give to certain situations before I am exhausted. This combined with a natural shyness (those who work with me are often shocked at this) can make social situations a nightmare for me. If I am meeting people somewhere in a social situation and I am travelling solo, I despise walking into a restaurant or bar to try to find them. My head is filled with irrational thoughts like "what if they're not there", "what if I fall over and flash my knickers as I walk in", "what if this isn't the right place" And so on. Ironically, when travelling solo and not meeting other people, I have no qualms about walking into a restaurant, sitting at a table for one and reading a book while having my dinner. I have a fear of being the butt of the joke, which is linked to being bullied as a child and this impacts me in social situations. The way to frame it is: a fear of being judged.

Conversely, in a professional setting, I will be the first to say hello, to introduce myself and make conversation. I flick the switch to let out the inner extrovert and no one would know that I am potentially uncomfortable on the inside.

So, how does this play out as an obstacle to being authentic? Simply put, there is a large social element to a work environment. You typically have colleagues, bosses, management and other people to interact with. You want to make a good impression and you may feel the urge to fit in. The challenge I personally have is that when 'work Sophie' is engaged, there is an appearance of confidence, self-assuredness and the ability to own or lead the room – the people I am working with will be completely unaware of the social awkwardness that I feel – and this means that at work social events there is a level of expectation for me to have the same persona as in the office, which is simply not the case.

I enjoy hanging out with work colleagues but large gatherings are torture for me, especially if there is a meal. My level of self-consciousness is heightened when faced with the likely chance of dropping food down my top while eating. I am also a morning person, so staying out until the early hours is just not for me, but you are rarely going to find yourself on a work social event at 10:00 am on a Saturday morning.

Ultimately, I do not want anyone I work with to think there is a false veneer that enables me to be seen as a confident person in the workplace – I do not want to be seen as inauthentic when I am anything but that. I can compartmentalise and separate parts of my persona to manage and succeed in the situation I am in. The best way to explain this is that my role as a subject matter expert (SME), combined with my experience, allows me to speak with a variety of colleagues across the business, to take charge, lead meetings and workshops, etc. To do this, I need to channel the inner extrovert to engage the associated confidence. If I allowed my natural shyness to take the driver's seat, I suspect I would not be as effective in challenging or confrontational situations – so when at work, I park that part of my personality until I am out of the office.

### Man-made heights

I have stood at the top of mountains and peered over the edge of a precipice without quaking knees or fear of heights. I have also had to be coaxed away from the wall to see the view from the top of the Rockefeller Centre in New York or have been clinging onto the tree on one of the platforms at Go Ape (a tree-top climbing adventure activity in the UK), sobbing with fear because I am scared the zip wire will break when I step off the ledge.

The problem is one of trust, although I have no idea where it came from. Out there in the wide world, Mother Nature created the mountains and they have barely moved for thousands of years. I trust her and I trust the ground. When it comes to man-made structures, I do not have the same assurances that the building will not fail. I worry that there is some form of defective concrete that will crumble when I stand on it, or that perhaps the bolts were not tightened enough and have worked their way loose just in time for me to fall from a great height.

This is, of course, irrational fear taking control, but in those moments, it is a difficult thing for me to manage. Sometimes, I literally need talking off the ledge at Go Ape because I am halfway round and I have to keep going and slide down the zip wire.

Sadly, this fear does come into the workplace on occasion and the fear is not necessarily just about the heights. As a woman working in a male-dominated environment, I have always felt the need to control and manage how I portray myself and how I am perceived – the balance between being respected or being seen as an over-emotional woman. This was something I needed to manage when working in one office building where the second-floor conference room 'hung' over the atrium and the floor of the conference room would literally shake as people walked up the stairs. I kid you not. You could literally feel the room and building move and this instantly kicked in my fear of man-made heights. I learned quickly where to sit or stand in the room to minimise the feeling of the floor shaking to try to manage my fear. In those early meetings when I was adjusting to the movement of the room, my colleagues could probably sense my fear, even though I tried to maintain an appearance of calm. I needed to share my fear without receiving one of those labels that would mark me as an over-emotional woman and 'weak'.

## *Acceptance and belonging*

As you will have already learned about me, I have always known that I am slightly different from the norm and this is something that I embrace. As a child, it was harder to embrace because being left out, isolated or ostracised was not something I (or anyone) would enjoy. I have my faults, as everyone does, but I try to be the best possible person I can be with a foundation of empathy, kindness and fairness. I have always had these foundations, so as a child when I was bullied, I could not fathom why I was disliked.

- Was I not friendly enough?
- Did I not get the jokes?
- Was my personality too much?
- Did I need to blend in more?
- Should I hide part of my personality to be liked more?
- Why do they like <insert name> more than me when we are very similar?
- If I had better clothes, would they like me more?
- If I do what they say or tell me to do, maybe then they will accept me?
- They have never spoken to me; how can they not like me?

These are examples of the questions that would cycle in my mind as a child. On occasion, some of these questions (and many more) still appear, unasked for.

The thing is that I am happy to stand out from the crowd, but there are times where a feeling of needing to belong would dominate my actions. However, after reading *Braving the Wilderness*[22] by Brené Brown, I realised that to belong, I first needed to accept myself. I needed to find that sense of belonging from within before I could seek a sense of belonging from anyone else. This, combined with a wealth of experience and maturity (as mature as I will ever be, anyway), has helped me understand that not everyone will like me in the same way as I will not like everyone I meet either, and that is OK.

| Tip: |
| :---: |
| **To belong, you first need to accept yourself.** |

## Fears from the wider world

Being afraid is not just about the internal fear that we experience, but also the fears that may exist due to external factors, including people. We have already spoken about the barriers to being authentic, which include the fear of rejection, but there is more to it than that, such as the fear of being:

- Humiliated;
- Ostracised;
- Isolated; or
- Not being accepted.

There is also fear of:

---

[22] *Braving the Wilderness: The Quest for True Belonging and the Courage to Stand Alone* by Brené Brown. Available at: https://www.amazon.co.uk/Braving-Wilderness-Quest-Belonging-Courage/dp/0812995848.

- Thunder-stealers;
- Narcissists;
- Bullies;
- Bigots;
- Misogynists;
- And more.

This second list, while different from the first, includes fears of things that could exist in your workplace that stop you from being yourself. For example, if the environment you work in regularly sees people taking credit for work they did not produce, how collaborative and open would you want to be? Of if there are people who dominate and suppress others, how would you feel about raising your hand to ask a question or provide an opposing view?

These lists could easily be expanded as there are many fears that may arise that hold us back from being who we truly are.

As we have spent time talking about internal fears, we will now delve a little deeper into the world of external fears with examples of when a decision has been needed to fight the fear and stand firm.

### Thunder-stealers

What is a 'thunder-stealer' in the workplace? In social circumstances, it is typically someone who overshadows your achievement or moment of joy with news of their own. An example of this can be found in the television series *Friends*, where Monica and Chandler get engaged and Monica feels as though Rachel steals her thunder by kissing Ross in the hallway. Monica feels this distracted the other members of the friendship group from what was a momentous occasion celebrating her engagement. This is similar in a work setting where often there is someone who needs to be the hero, leads the narrative or takes credit for the work of others without sharing the recognition or acknowledging the contribution of others.

I have more experiences than I would like to recall where someone has taken credit for the work I have produced or where someone has presented my idea as their own, but here are some examples to illustrate thunder-stealers at work:

- **The one where your manager takes all the credit**

  In a previous role, despite limited experience in the subject, I was tasked with writing the company's information security policy and associated documentation. This was a prerequisite for the company obtaining its international standard, ISO 27001, accreditation. I do not have a background in information security, but I did my best. When complete, I shared it with my line manager. It needed to be presented to the senior leadership to get approval for it to go live, and then be cascaded to the wider business.

  I was not present in the meeting but I was told what happened by one of the other senior leaders. My boss had opened his part of the meeting by talking about the information security policy that *he* had written, with no mention of who actually wrote the policy. Thankfully for me, and awkwardly for him, one of the senior leaders present knew that I was the one who wrote the policy. In an unintentional show of allyship, the senior leader interrupted him when he took credit for my work and said, "I believe Sophie wrote that," which made my boss correct his statement.

I had not known for sure that this manager was the type to pass off the work of others as his own, but now I knew that he was not going to be an ally and champion me or the team.

- **The one where your peer passes the work off as their own in front of you**

An experience of plagiarism occurred during an engagement to support a large client with multiple subsidiaries to mature their service management practices. I had spent time with one of the other service management managers, walking them through the approach I use for incident-prioritisation matrices, service models, etc. I have a draft of documentation like this, authored by me, ready prepared for when I am working with clients, that I have honed and perfected over the years. I sent a number of documents through for their reference, all of which was branded and was clearly my intellectual property.

About a week later, I was in a regular meeting with the area of the business I was supporting, including the manager I had met with. The topic of conversation was what progress we had each made for maturing the service management approaches and ensuring there was alignment across the group. To my surprise, the other area manager presented his screen and the work he had done on the incident priorities and service models. What he was presenting was literally the information I had shared with him with an extra couple of words in it, but ultimately it was my work being presented back to me without any recognition.

Now, to be clear, I did not need praise for my work here, but it was an interesting moment. I was being shown my own work with no comment about collaboration or where the detail had come from. To add to the moment, the team I was working closely with who were on the call were messaging me at the same time. They had recognised that the work being presented was mine and that the manager was illegitimately taking credit for it.

- **The one with the major-incident hero**

    Picture the scene – you are running a major incident and you are close to finding the solution with all the necessary teams involved and your stakeholders have been informed every step of the way. There is one person in the engineering team who is notorious for jumping in at the last minute to 'save the day' and claim the glory of resolving the incident. (If you have ever read *The Phoenix Project*[23] by Gene Kim, Kevin Behr and George Spafford, you will recognise the character Brent here.)

---

[23] *The Phoenix Project: A Novel about IT, DevOps, and Helping Your Business Win* by Gene Kim, Kevin Behr and George Spafford. Available at: *https://www.amazon.co.uk/Phoenix-Project-DevOps-Helping-Business/dp/0988262592*.

But this is not happening this time – everyone is working cohesively together, and the end is almost in sight.

Or so you thought. The engineer known for last-minute 'save-the-day' antics jumps on the major incident conference call and says, "It's OK, I fixed it and it's working now." Being the consummate professional that you are, you do not ask the question "what did you do and why did you do it alone without engaging in the major incident", even though you really want to. Instead, you keep your cool, ask them what they did to fix the incident and how they have confirmed that it is working. Your question is answered in a glib, gloating manner that glosses over the technical details along with the announcement that this engineer bypassed the major-incident communications channels and went straight to the internal customers to confirm resolution.

Not only is this incredibly frustrating, it is also a typical display of hero behaviour that does not prompt teamwork or present a cohesive image of the technology function to the wider business. A major incident, when managed effectively, is a team effort. It involves colleagues from throughout the technology function, and the wider business, coming together in an epic display of collaboration. The rogue, cavalier approach is self-serving. It can prevent others from sharing their thoughts or acting proactively, for fear of being made to look foolish by this type of behaviour.

- **The one where a peer rewrites the past**

You have left your previous organisation and are on to your next opportunity. You thoroughly enjoyed the previous role, but felt it was time to spread your wings and move on. You, the organisation and your colleagues have parted ways amicably and with the best intentions. You have settled in to the new role and have a catch-up with your old team to see how they are getting on and generally see them in a social setting.

During the catch-up, one of your old team tells you about someone you used to work with who is claiming to have jointly implemented the service models YOU defined. You reply that the person who is making this claim is a nice person but appears to have rewritten the past. You know this to be true because they did not work at the company when you defined, agreed and implemented the service models.

Thankfully, your old team members know this already and are as amused as you, but when it comes to those who do not know you or have joined the organisation after you left, they will not realise this is a false narrative, so will take it to be factually correct. What does this mean for you? For who you are? Do you say something, or do you let it go?

There are further types of thunder-stealers, such as the people who posture in meetings to make themselves look good to the senior leaders. Outside of the meeting, they are more amenable, or are supportive in one-to-one conversations but not vocal in front of the wider group. Unfortunately, these thunder-stealers exist in daily life and there may be no escape, but that does not mean to say that you need to let these people hold you back.

## *Narcissists*

Oh, how we love the narcissist, but maybe not as much as they love themselves. These are the people who must be the hero/heroine in their own story and may not have the self-awareness to understand that not everything is about them. These people can be tricky to navigate. When dealing with a narcissist, you have to find a way (or ways) to influence them and placate them without pandering to them. For example, when I am trying to give feedback to someone who has narcissistic tendencies, I know they may not respond well to constructive feedback. I use the 'compliment sandwich' and deliver the constructive feedback in between layers of positive, affirming feedback. In this circumstance, I am managing the wider situation too as I would prefer to deliver the feedback without conflict.

When it comes to being authentic and the fear of these individuals impacting or impeding your ability to be who you are, it is important to remember that your goal is not to bend to the will of others, but to be comfortable in your own skin. Allowing your personality to shine, to embrace your persona and reduce the amount of masking you may be doing to 'fit in'. The narcissist is going to be more concerned about themselves than they are you – although there may be times where they will be concerned about how you or your image may impact them if your authentic self does not align with their vision.

I am going to be blunt here: if this circumstance arises, it is totally a THEM problem and NOT a YOU problem. In a world of over 8 billion humans, none of us are the same. We are all individuals. Though we may share traits and beliefs, we are still unique and, as such, should embrace our individuality.

## *Bullies*

I have experienced bulling at school, college, university, in relationships and in the workplace. How I have managed each of the bullying situations has differed as I have grown and matured. There have been times where I have bent my will to fit in. Times where I have smiled and nodded. Times where I have appeared compliant but have fought back in the shadows. And the times where I have stood my ground to confront the bully. It is my belief that there is not a 'one size fits all' approach to dealing with a bully, but there are a variety of factors that you are likely to take into consideration, such as:

- Where you are (physical location);
- What the situation is;
- Who the bully/aggressor is;
- What you are being bullied about; and
- Who you are (are you protecting yourself and others?).

I would love to say that the way to go about it is to stand up to the bully every time, to call them out and have the confrontation. But I have not always done this myself. My mum always told me to pick my battles, and this is something I always consider, regardless of the circumstances.

What about the fear of being bullied and how that impacts your ability/desire/goal to be authentically you? If this question resonates with you, then you also need to consider what being authentic, and allowing yourself to unfurl those wings to be the butterfly that you are, means to you. Bullies exist. This is a fact. It is not right and it is certainly not OK. Their reasoning for behaving in such an abhorrent manner is not something that I can comprehend and these are not shoes I would like to walk in. At the same time, I do know that bullies bully for a variety of reasons, such as:

- Wanting to dominate others;
- Wanting to improve their social or professional standing;
- Having low self-esteem and wanting to feel better about themselves; or
- Using bullying as a coping mechanism for trauma.

This list could go on. The point here is that understanding that these types of people exist is important in your recognition that sometimes things are not fair in life, but that does not mean you give up or stop. You are in control of your own destiny and, as such, get to decide how much you will let a bully deter you from being who you are. As with the narcissist, if they do not like who and how you are as an individual, that is definitely NOT a YOU problem!

### *Misogynists and bigots*

We will encounter these people whether we want to or not. There is no escaping antiquated views of the world and the individuals who think a woman's place is in the home or doing those stereotypical 'pink' tasks. It is a sad fact that more than 70% of women in England have experienced misogyny in the workplace according to *Family Friendly Working* article from 2023.[24]

If I had penny or pound for each time I have been the subject of a misogynistic comment or sexist remark, I would be incredibly rich. From being asked to make the tea or coffee, to making the notes in a meeting room full of men, or being told that women are inherently better at admin because of their biological make-up or that I am a dumb blonde – these are just a sample of thing things said to me.

The point here is that misogyny is something that we have to deal with. Yes, it is annoying. Yes, it should not be a thing. Yes, the world would be a better place if equity truly existed, but sadly we are not there yet. It is my hope that future generations will be able to eradicate sexism and this way of thinking, but unfortunately, this is definitely not the world I live in. As such, you have to find ways to cope with it. Again, you should not have to, but there it is.

To manage these situations, you have to find a way to deal with them that aligns your values and who you are without lowering yourself to the level of someone behaving poorly. Personally, I find that one of the following helps me in those circumstances where someone is behaving in a way that does not align with the organisation's values (or with employment laws such as discrimination, bullying in the workplace, etc.):

- A stoic or bored expression on my face with no retort (I recognise that this is not necessarily adult behaviour but it helps me survive in some situations);

---

[24] *https://www.familyfriendlyworking.co.uk/2023/03/24/more-than-70-of-women-in-england-have-experienced-misogyny-at-work-a-new-survey-has-found.*

- A suitable sarcastic retort that highlights that I heard what was said but disagree and would like the person to retract or rethink their comment;
- An outright response contradicting the comments and calling out the bad behaviour;
- Speaking to the person privately to do the above;
- Ignoring the comment; or
- A dash of well-placed passive aggressive body language like a yawn, a raised eyebrow, walking away, etc.

The same applies to bigotry, xenophobic or any other discriminatory behaviour. More often than not, taking the wind out of someone's sails by not replying or rising to the bait is the biggest response you can give.

The additional point here is that when someone is behaving poorly to you, for whatever reason, you have the power to decide if and how you are going to respond. If you do choose to respond, this is in your time frame and no one else's.

If these kinds of people are a reason why you are holding back from being truly authentic, it is worth spending time performing self-reflection to understand why this is the case. If it involves specific individuals, consider who they are to you, what it means if you are confronted with their poor behaviour when you have been yourself, and what it will mean if you are yourself and they do not like it. Some of the answers to these thoughts may result in a "this is not a ME problem" realisation.

It is worth adding that if any of these things are being experienced by anyone, there are probably systems and processes to deal with these issues, especially in the workplace. Consider exploring your options and report any misbehaviour through the proper channels, such as the HR department.

**Other fears that may exist**

Before moving on, it is worth saying that there are likely to be many more fears associated with being authentic along with a myriad of reasons why you have these fears. While this book may not specifically go into a fear that resonates with you, hopefully, the approach of taking a step back to reflect and understand the 'why' behind the fear will help you overcome those things that are holding you back.

> **Tip:**
>
> **You have to understand what you're afraid of before you can tackle or overcome it.**

**Challenge the fear to a duel**

It is time to talk about how to fight these fears and the ways you can do it, so then you can focus on authenticity.

First things first. There is no right nor wrong way to tackle fear as a general rule.

Each person will have a different approach, and it may take a few attempts to overcome a fear. There may also be times where the barrier to overcoming your fear feels so vast that you learn to accept and adapt – although, in my case, this is reserved for spiders and moths (which is a whole different book!).

In the world of service management and process management, there is a process called 'continual improvement', which needs you to start where you are, taking stock of the current situation before making changes.

When it comes to challenging the fear to a duel and fighting that fear, you need to do the same thing, and there are some basic steps you can follow:

## Understanding your fear

In order to face something, you need to know what it is you are facing before taking the next step. What is it that you are afraid of? What is it that is stopping you from being yourself? Are there any specific reasons why you are not able to be your authentic self?

Spending time delving into what is holding you back is going to be important to not only understand the 'what' but also the 'why'? What makes it a fear? What is the worst thing that can happen as a result of you being true to yourself? Are there any repercussions or potential repercussions, and if so, what are they? Can you use reason and logic to add some rationality to these potential repercussions?

## Take bite-sized chunks

You can make slow, progressive changes to embrace your true authentic self. You can gradually make changes at a rate and pace that you are comfortable with.

I do not generally wear a lot of make-up and only learned how to do it in my mid-thirties. When I start working for a client full-time, particularly when in the office, I tend to wear a full face of make-up, every day, as part of the mask while I am building relationships with people. As time passes, the amount of make-up I wear will decrease to the bare minimum or none at all.

I love wearing trainers. They are super comfortable and I have lots of different ones in different colours. When I started going to conferences and events, I would also wear shoes or boots (which I also love, but not as much), ensuring that I was portraying the 'right' professional image. This was typically paired with jeans and a smart top. I do not do that anymore unless I feel inclined to. Instead, I wear my trainers and they are usually colour-coordinated with something else I am wearing. The trainers go with the jeans and a top nicely and I am still portraying a professional image, while making sure I am comfortable in my own skin (and feet).

### *Mind over matter*

I am generally not a fan of the expression 'mind over matter' for a variety of reasons. Often, because it is not as simple as telling yourself to "get a grip" or to "strap on your brave pants" and then push through whatever it is that is holding you back. Certainly, this is very true for me when it comes to reaching out to grab a bar of chocolate when I am no longer hungry, but the sugar craving is stronger than my willpower. However, there is a lot to be said for reframing your thoughts, which is a form of 'mind over matter'.

"What is reframing?" I hear you ask. It is taking a negative viewpoint and flipping the perspective to be a positive or empowering viewpoint instead. For example, instead of saying "I'm scared, and I cannot do this", you can reframe the sentence to "I'm afraid but I will try, because it may work out OK". Rather than a mindset of "people will laugh at me" or make negative comments, reframing turns that around to be "people might like my ideas or my approach". There are going to be circumstances where you may not always get the response you hope for, but if you never try and do not put yourself in the position for a positive outcome, you will never know.

Instead of thinking about what could go wrong, why not try thinking about what could go right! Try visualising success and positive outcomes rather than failure or negative outcomes.

This is not always an easy thing to do and there are circumstances where the fear will take over. In those situations, pause afterwards and reflect to understand what happened, how you felt and consider if there is anything you could have done to push through the fear. All while remembering to be kind to yourself if the fear overwhelmed you.

**Tip:**
**Learning how to reframe a perspective or point of view is powerful and can be a game changer!**

### *Breathe and stay in the moment*

In the last four years, I have actively sought out opportunities to speak in public, be it at conferences, webinars, on podcasts, etc., with the goal of pushing myself outside of my comfort zone to share some of my knowledge and experiences. Without exception, at every event I have been part of, I have felt stage fright resulting in physical responses such as my heart racing and pounding in my chest, sweaty palms, shallow breathing heading towards hyperventilating and the case of the 'nervous wee' (needing the bathroom multiple times before getting on the stage). Thankfully, I have also learned the power of deep breathing, particularly box breathing, to help calm down my nervous system.

If you have not heard of boxing breathing, this is what you do:

1. Inhale for a count of 4

4. Hold for a count of 4

2. Hold for a count of 4

3. Exhale for a count of 4

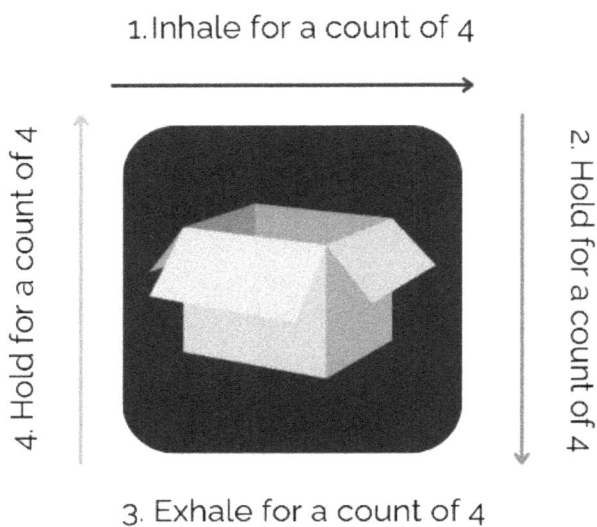

**Figure 8: Boxing Breathing**

1. Inhale for a count of four.
2. Hold the breath in for a count of four.
3. Exhale for a count of four.
4. Hold for a count of four, and then repeat the process.

The first couple of rounds of this breathing will feel weird, particularly if your breathing is ragged and the fear is taking hold, but stick with it. After two or three rounds, you will feel your heartbeat begin to slow down to a normal rate, the sweaty palms will be slightly less sticky, and you will feel a degree of calm washing over you.

There are, of course, other breathing techniques and things you can do to help you find a sense of calm, such as yoga and meditation, with many resources available to you (check out the appendix for useful links).

## Take the leap

Here is a quote from Mark Twain that perfectly summarises courage and taking the leap:

> *"Courage is not the lack of fear.*
> *It is acting in spite of it."*

Stepping out to the front of a stage to deliver a session in public is one of the ways I push my boundaries and fight back against the fear. There are times when I can feel my knees knocking, my hands shaking and I think "why on earth am I putting myself through this". Then I realise it is because it is part of who I am to share, to speak with others and in order for me to continue to be my authentic self, I need to push through that giant wall of stage fright to speak to an audience.

For me, stepping against the tide of fear helps me break through it – perhaps the same will work for you.

## Hindsight is a wonderful thing

Hindsight is a wonderful thing, but it is important not to get caught in the trap of dwelling on the past. Instead, learn from your experiences and use those lessons to help inform your decision making.

What is it that you need to do to keep driving yourself forwards to being the fully authentic you? What are those fears from the past that are trying to control the now and the future? What has happened when you have tried before – is there something you can take away from previous experiences that will give you insight into how to navigate forwards and push through the fear?

The past is gone, you cannot change it, so look back to learn and then face the now, focus your energies on what is next and where you are right now.

> **Tip:**
> **Hindsight is a wonderful thing, but it is important not to get caught in the trap of dwelling on the past.**

### *You are not alone*

It may feel like it, but you are not alone. There will be people who have either been in a similar position or those who can empathise with you, possibly offering you support. Or maybe just a friendly ear for you to share your concerns and help you work through the fear to see what to do next.

Each person's path is their own, but there will be shared experiences and shared fears. Perhaps talking out your situation will result in advice or options you had not considered before.

If you have a mentor, maybe ask their opinion. If you do not have a mentor, perhaps it is worth getting one and asking for help (we will talk about mentoring later on in the book).

If you have friends, colleagues, significant others or family members whom you can confide in, then get those fears out.

Being authentic can be hard if your fears are taking over, but with the support of those around you – people you trust – then perhaps you will be able to show that fear who the boss is!

## 5: What are you afraid of?

Before we head into the next chapter, focusing on influence and the power it holds, remember that it is perfectly OK to be concerned and fearful about being your authentic self. Particularly so if your fear is linked to any of the barriers to being authentic. This is normal and at one stage or another, we will all have felt something similar. Your feelings are valid. The key is pushing that fear aside as much as possible to continue your journey, driving forwards to being comfortable in your own skin and being authentic.

# CHAPTER 6: BREAKING OUT THE INFLUENCING GUNS

> **The power of positive influence. Knowing yourself and others and using your skills to drive change.**

In this chapter, we are going to talk about influence and how that can support you on your journey to being your authentic self. It may seem like the two things are not connected when you first think about it, but there is a lot to be said for building an environment around you that enables you to be yourself – and to do this, you may need to break out your influencing guns.

We will start with talking about what is meant by 'influence' and then how this can support you on your journey to being authentic.

Quite often, there is a misconception between influence and manipulation. We will address this straight off with the definitions of the two words from Dictionary.com:

- *"**Influence** = the capacity or power of persons of things to be a compelling force on or produce effects on the actions, behaviour, opinions, etc. of others*
- ***Manipulate** = to manage or influence skilfully, especially in an unfair manner"*

While there are links between the two in the definition, the key difference is that to manipulate is to influence in a negative or unfair manner, often for nefarious reasons. To influence is typically to encourage, to help direct people in the right direction, and so on.

For me personally, working in an environment that is positive and accepting is key to being able to be my authentic self in the workplace. It is not a given that this kind of environment exists and often, I need to help create a space that enables me and others to be authentic. I use my stakeholder-management and influencing skills to achieve this. I spend time getting to know the people around me to understand them and how they operate in their environment. I try to find commonalities and mutual areas of interest/values/opinions, etc. All of this helps make an environment that is positive and open to authenticity.

These are the realms of positive influence and nowhere near the dark side of manipulation. You are creating a mutually supportive environment that not only allows you to be you, but also the people around you to be themselves, too. Although your motive may be to find that space or landing site for you, it should also be about the wider community or team. If you find yourself veering to the darker side of influencing, then it will be important to pause. Spend time reflecting on and analysing the approach you are taking to ensure it is aligned with your values and what you are trying to achieve. If it is not aligned with your values and has a negative undertone, then my advice would always be to stop. Take a step back and consider reframing your approach to one that benefits more than you.

**There is power in positive influence**

In a previous role, I had the opportunity to attend a programme of workshops hosted by Chartwell Learning & Development Ltd, focusing on "Positive Power and

Influence" which was fascinating. Also in attendance were the other members of the technology senior leadership team, which was insightful. The purpose of attending these workshops was to build on our stakeholder-management skills and to support us on our journey to raise the profile of the technology function in the wider business.

During the programme, we went through a series of activities and roleplay exercises. The intended outcome was to help us understand the differing ways to influence, including push-and-pull techniques, listening and replaying, and positive and negative assertion. It is definitely a  programme worth investing in, particularly if you are in a role where you need to engage with stakeholders who are challenging, who are maybe stuck in their ways, or to drive continual improvement in an environment that is resistant to change.

Here are some ways that you can employ positive influence on those around you:

### *Lead by example*

- Model the behaviours you want to see in others.
- Show your acceptance of others, in a judgement-free environment.
- Create a psychologically safe environment for your teams.
- Set an example for your team, your peers and senior leadership.

### *Relationship-building*

- Build connection .
- Empathise.

- Find common ground and interests.
- Invest time in both building and strengthening relationships.

### Inspire and motivate

- Share the vision and purpose – the 'why'.
- Bring people on the journey. Remember, no one wants to be 'done to'.
- Let them know where they are heading and what the benefits are.

### Positive communication

- Use uplifting language and positive reinforcement.
- Give constructive feedback (Radical Candor – a book which is about being honest and clear without being rude or cruel).[25]
- Avoid gossip, dwelling on negativity or harsh criticism.
- Create feedback loops.

### Empower, encourage and motivate

- Be the tower of strength.
- Give people the tools they need to fly solo.
- Big them up, build their confidence.
- Allow and accept failure with a culture of continual learning and improvement.

---

[25] *Radical Candor*: *https://www.radicalcandor.com/.*

### *Be curious and listen*

- Ask questions and listen to the answers.
- Aim to understand and seek common ground.
- Seek opinions and feedback.
- Learn, grow, develop yourself and those around you.

### *Be vulnerable and share stories*

- Share your journey.
- Show you are human and fallible.
- Find a way to express yourself in a relatable way.
- Do not be afraid to say you do not know or that you need support.

### Raising your profile

Your profile is born from your personal brand.

Your personal brand is the story you tell your professional community, potential employers, your teams, etc. It is your calling card and the thing that sets you apart from your peers and the competition, showcasing not only what you do, but how you do it and why. There are some basic elements of a personal brand: values, skills, strengths, your style and voice, your reputation and your presence (both in person and virtually). All these things combined make up the package of you that you then need to make visible to raise your profile.

> **Tip:**
> Your profile and personal brand are like a calling card, stating who you are and setting you apart from your peers.

## *What is raising your profile?*

In the context of this book, it is not about filling out details in LinkedIn or creating a professional Instagram account. It is about self-promotion, marketing yourself and your strengths to your network, potential employers and the wider professional community. To do this, there is an element of positive influence that you need to employ.

When we talk about self-promotion, do not confuse this with boasting, arrogance or an inflated sense of self. What you are aiming to do is to let the wider world know that you are there, what you can do, how you do it and why working with you is not only going to add value to them as an individual but also to the organisation. It is a realisation of your limitations but also confidence in your abilities to make a difference.

One of my favourite interview questions to answer as the candidate is: "What are your strengths and weaknesses?" The reason I love being asked this question is that I see my "weaknesses" as development opportunities. They are areas for growth, evolution and improvement where my aim is to make them a strength also. When it comes to raising your profile, there is power in acknowledging failures, development areas or topics where you want to learn more. On social media, I have openly posted when I have failed an exam because it is part of my values to be honest, to share that sometimes I find exams incredibly hard (even when I am a subject matter expert for the exam I have taken), to show vulnerability and to accept that for me, taking an exam fills me with dread.

Last night, I was talking with my daughter and one of her friends. The friend has recently entered the workplace through a degree apprenticeship and is the only one of the friendship group to do so – which means her friendship group may not be able to fully relate with her experience of working in an office five days a week and the etiquette associated with it. During our conversation, she spoke about not knowing how to handle positive feedback from colleagues and members of the leadership team, with a tendency to say "thank you" but then to say "it's just my job" or "well, I didn't do it all by myself", or something that would unintentionally diminish or deflect the positive feedback.

Instantly, my response to her was talking about raising your profile, how important it is to accept the feedback without anything that could potentially negate the compliment, as it is OK to just say "thank you, I appreciate you saying that". It is perfectly acceptable to acknowledge you did something well without having to make yourself smaller in some way. If this fills you with dread, then perhaps you could add: "Is there anything I could have done better for next time, or any learning areas to help me continue to improve?" Being open to coaching and appearing coachable is a great way to raise your profile too – especially during your early career. I also spoke about how this kind of feedback is the first stepping stone to raising your profile in the workplace.

One of her concerns was about coming across like she was boasting or taking credit where it was not due. I explained that for someone to go to the lengths of providing her the feedback, then it is obviously work that deserved to be recognised and should be accepted without the additional "but" or diminishing the statement following the "thank you". To illustrate my point, I told her what my typical introduction is when I am speaking at an event or writing a profile for something I am involved in. When finished, I asked her if it sounded like I was boasting or being arrogant – a loaded question really, but I was keen to understand her perspective. She replied, "It sounds like you are selling yourself and showing what you are capable of." Which was exactly the point.

Raising your profile is self-promotion. It is accepting the positive feedback and recognition of a job well done and not being ashamed to talk about it. It is about taking professional pride for the work you do and having the confidence in your ability to deliver it.

### *How do you raise your profile?*

There is no one way to do this, and it will differ from person to person on the best approach to take, such as the following:

- Build your personal brand
  - We have just spoken about the importance of this in the previous section, but define your expertise, values, etc.
  - Make sure your LinkedIn profile and other professional profiles reflect your brand and what you stand for.
- Use your voice and share opinions
  - Use social media platforms such as LinkedIn to post meaningful or thought-provoking content.
  - Respond to insightful posts from others.
  - Attend webinars and conferences – get involved, ask questions.
  - Be visible in meetings – offer solutions, provide advice and support.
- Networking and strategic relationships

- o Reach out to mentors, peers or people in leadership roles – asking for advice or offering support.
- o Join professional bodies or communities and get involved.
- o Collaborate with others on their initiatives.
- Highlight achievements (without bragging)
  - o Share learnings and how they can support others.
  - o Use things like the STAR method[26] in your LinkedIn posts to explain the situation, task, actions and results.
  - o Talk about outcomes and not individual activities.
  - o Storytelling is a way to make your experiences memorable, relatable, emotionally compelling and help others connect with and remember you.
  - o Admit weaknesses and limitations. Actively seek learning opportunities.
- Keep developing yourself
  - o Attend training courses.
  - o Obtain certifications that support your expertise.
  - o Remember that personal development is a continual journey throughout your life – is there such as a thing as the 'finished article'?
- Support the development of others
  - o Become a mentor.
  - o Volunteer.
  - o Speak at conferences and on panels.

---

[26] *https://www.ddiworld.com/solutions/behavioral-interviewing/star-method.*

- o Offer training and support to others.
- Engage with the media – podcasts and articles/blogs
  - o Contribute to the community through the platforms of others.
  - o Seek out opportunities to write blogs or articles for industry-respected organisations (even if for free!).

Something that I often do in the workplace is engage with the senior leadership team to find out what they are working towards and see how the work I do in my role can support them on their journey. I like to have regular meetings with them to keep the conversation going. By 'regular', I typically mean once a quarter, as anyone working in the C-suite will have an incredibly busy diary to compete with, so I want to show an interest in supporting them without becoming a burden.

There is an informal framework in the tech industry – the CIO's 3-2-1 rule for strategic enablement – which reframes the technology function from being a service provider to a strategy enabler. Its purpose is to align more effectively with the wider business. It is an adaptation of the classic 3-2-1 rule commonly used for data backup, which has been reimaged for CIOs to support a better alignment with the organisational strategy and foster a focus on business value.

In a nutshell, you do the following:

- Focus on **3 strategic technology initiatives** that align with the organisation's top priorities (e.g. growth, efficiency and innovation). Delivering value through business outcomes as well as IT ones.
- Build **2 cross-functional partnerships** with key business units – one internal-facing (e.g. finance, HR,

etc.) and one external-facing (e.g. marketing, customer services, etc.). The aim is to co-create value and embed the technology function as a partner throughout the business.

- Define **1 "North Star" metric**, that is, a single, business-focused metric that the technology function supports. Demonstrating the success of the technology function contributing to a strategic business outcome that the CEO and board members both understand, and care about.

This is a technology-focused analogy, but the approach can be used by any team in the organisation. You can adapt it to aim for co-creation of value and to support the goal of raising both your profile and that of your team and the wider department.

Until you try raising your profile, you have no idea what benefits you could reap from it. Sometimes, you will be more successful than you imagine and at other times, you will just plod along happily. Regardless, it is an important part of your authenticity journey to understand how, and when, to raise your profile in the workplace.

As a woman working in technology, I have found it incredibly important and beneficial to raise my profile to challenge stereotypes and any potential discrimination as well as to maintain my position among my peers. While I cannot comment on what the challenges are for men in the workplace, I can say that to get a seat at the table in a male-dominated industry, I have had to continually fight for that seat and do so through raising my profile, competence and credibility, proving repeated value and using positive influence where necessary.

## Be assertive. Your opinion counts

You have been employed to share your expertise and skills with the organisation you work for. To do this, you need to speak up and voice your opinions, your ideas, potential solutions, etc. You should do this in meetings and discussions with your colleagues REGARDLESS of the position they hold in the company. And, regardless of the experience or position you hold within your organisation, you have value to add. There is a book about the co-creation of value in organisations which talks about collaboration, understanding your environment and how using knowledge management can create and sustain value.[27] You should not be afraid to assert yourself and voice your opinion.

Even a CEO who has progressed to the most senior position in the organisation will not have all the answers. They may have been in your role in the past, but time has passed, and technology moves on. This means they may not be as close to the 'action' as you are, so your opinion matters to them. If it does not, there is a question about the type of leader they are, but that is a whole other book. You may not have a direct line to the senior leaders, but you do have access to your manager and senior management. There is nothing wrong with raising a hand and saying, "I have something to add here."

---

[27] *Co-creating value in organizations with ITIL 4: a guide for consultants, executives and managers* by David Barrow. Available at: *https://www.amazon.co.uk/Co-creating-value-organizations-ITIL-consultants/dp/0113318510.*

Being assertive is not always easy. Especially in the earlier stages of your career, or if you are naturally shy or introverted. It can be incredibly daunting to raise your hand and share your thoughts in a meeting or an open forum. There is also nothing wrong with putting your hand up and asking questions. In all likelihood, others will have the same or similar questions, so do not be afraid to ask. There are ways to get your opinion out there without pushing your boundaries to the point of discomfort, such as the following:

- If you are in a virtual meeting, there are options where you can raise a hand to alert the people in the room that you have something to say. Typically, when you do this, the room will follow common courtesy and allow you to speak, uninterrupted, to share your thoughts or point of view.
- If you are in an in-person meeting, there are typically moments where there is a gap or the floor is opened to the wider attendees to ask questions or make suggestions. In these circumstances, you have an opportunity to put yourself out there.
- If doing either of the above is something that is difficult for you or you are more of a reflector who prefers to raise a point after the meeting you can:
  - Send an email providing your thoughts with an offer for a smaller meeting to discuss further; or
  - Arrange a meeting to discuss further and share your thoughts in a smaller setting.

I am 47 years old at the time of writing this book and have been working full-time for 25 years. When I am in a meeting and have something to contribute, I still feel my heartbeat quicken with nerves, sweaty palms and dash of anxiety associated with not wanting to look like an idiot for speaking up, but I do it anyway. I work very hard to portray an air of confidence and extroversion, which explains why people are often surprised when I tell them I get nervous in meetings or before public speaking. However, it is something I work very hard to conquer because it is intrinsically linked to raising my profile, asserting myself and continuing to build my personal brand.

What does this have to do with authenticity? Everything and nothing all at once. Part of my authenticity is to be open and honest with those around me about when I get nervous or shy, about the aspects of my personality that may not be obvious in a professional setting. I want to support others on their journey to authenticity and to do this, I have to potentially be more vulnerable and transparent.

**You cannot please everyone**

One thing I am often heard saying is that the most challenging aspect about any role I have filled is people. At the same time, though, the most rewarding aspect of any role is working with people. It is a duality that goes hand in hand. I appreciate the irony here.

What does that mean when it comes to authenticity and how does influencing fit into this piece of the puzzle? Simply put, you need to understand who you are working with, your teams, your colleagues, your peers, and the leadership team, so that you can learn how authenticity is accepted and enabled where you work. It is important to recognise that not everyone will appreciate authenticity and your version of it.

Let us start with the following simple truth.

## 6: Breaking out the influencing guns

You do not go to work to make friends. You go to work to fulfil a role, to progress your career and to earn a living. Making friends at work is a pleasant side effect but not a necessity. Please do not misunderstand me here, it is of course better to have an amicable, positive working environment. But you do not need to become besties with your co-workers. And this is, of course, a two-way street.

The world we live in is made up of different people, cultures, ways of working, beliefs, interests, etc. It is therefore likely that you will meet people who are not your 'cup of tea'. It is unlikely that you will like everyone you meet, and that is OK. The same thing applies the other way round. You may not be everyone's 'cup of tea' either. And that is also OK. It is not always easy to accept when other people may not like you, but it is a fact. From a work perspective, what do you do about this?

- Do you go on a charm offensive?
- Do you change parts of your personality to become more likeable to that other person?
- Do you ignore them and think "stuff it, they don't like me so I won't bother with them"?

No, you use your stakeholder-management and influencing skills. What you are working towards is a mutually acceptable collaboration or compromise that allows you to work with the other person without any conflict. Unfortunately, it may be that the other person does not want to be in a cohesive environment, in which case you need to break out those influencing guns to defuse a challenging or confrontational relationship at work.

How do you do this? Firstly, it is worth noting that it may not be about you specifically. There could be a whole host of reasons why someone is behaving or reacting in a cold, detached or impersonal way. This is where empathy really plays a part. Personally, I find the single most effective way to build a rapport with someone who I may find challenging, is to start learning more about them, by being curious. It is often most effective to work from a place of commonality or recognition of the other person's motivation than to go in blindly with the assumption that they simply do not like you. This is basic reframing of your perspective on the situation, which we spoke about in the previous chapter.

Learning about someone and being curious does not mean peppering them with a million questions in one go – this will be annoying for anyone and likely to damage an already tenuous relationship. Instead of this, during the course of a normal conversation with the stakeholder, ask them a few questions to get their opinion and to make them the focal point of the conversation. If you disagree with their point of view, in this first instance of being inquisitive, it is advisable to say things like "oh, that's an interesting point of view" or "I can see what you're saying there". The reason for not openly disagreeing at this point is because your aim here is to build rapport with them, not to further fuel any dislike or distance between you.

This approach is a gradual one that needs to be nurtured over time. The caveat is to only do this if you are truly interested in building a better rapport with the individual. If you have no interest and it will not cause you any issues in the workplace, your decision point here is whether you want to bother making the effort.

When I was working as a service desk manager, there was a particular stakeholder that I just could not seem to get on with. They had made it clear that they were not a fan of mine through the words they used, their tone and their body language. I also could not place my finger on why I was not their biggest fan either, but there was just something that seemed to rub me up the wrong way. Whether it was when logging tickets with my service desk or escalations or how they interacted with me in meetings, it was just clear that we were not going to be friends. It was a mutual "you're not my kind of person".

Dave[28] was often rude and dismissive of me in public. We both worked in the same part of the open office and there were occasions where he took the opportunity to poke fun at or ridicule me, but in a sarcastic, unpleasant manner that did not fall within the typical office 'banter'. I thought I had done a relatively good job of masking my aversion to this person – after all, I had worked in technical support roles for over a decade and having to deal with customers who were not my cup of tea was a regular occurrence. However, one day one of my team commented: "Sophie, it's really obvious that you don't like Dave. Even when you're trying to hide it."

I was shocked that my poker face and masking had failed completely. I was also ashamed, because if my mask had slipped, then perhaps my behaviour was less than

---

[28] Dave is not his real name.

professional[29] and could have unintentionally hurt Dave's feelings. I may not have liked the guy, but I would never intentionally hurt someone's feelings.

I performed some self-reflection and checked in with my values, realising how I had not been living according to my values and needed to adjust my behaviour. More from a personal standpoint than anything, but also with the recognition that if I had been obvious in my opinion of someone, then I was not showing myself in the best professional light. I made the decision to adjust my behaviour, to reframe my approach to one of curiosity and to make an effort to be kind.

I deployed the stakeholder-management skill of being curious to build rapport. At first, it was met with mistrust. I knew that my mask had failed with Dave and I understood his response. I persevered and maintained a polite, professional approach combined with curiosity and over time, a better rapport evolved between me and Dave. He was still often rude or dismissive of me in public, but I did not allow the behaviour to incite a reciprocal response from me. Dave's behaviour and how it was perceived was not my concern. My concern was correcting my behaviour and aligning myself with my values, maintaining my professionalism in the workplace. It is fair to say that I typically lead with empathy, but in this case specifically, I did not know the motivators for Dave to behave as he did – there could have been reasons wholly unrelated to me.

---

[29] While Dave was often rude and dismissive of me in public, that was not an excuse for me to respond with equally unprofessional behaviour.

## 6: Breaking out the influencing guns

By the time I left the organisation, my relationship with Dave had improved, certainly from my perspective, and I had learned a valuable lesson. Not everyone will like you and you will not like everyone, but that is no reason to diminish your professionalism, as it is a reflection of you, your values and your authentic self.

# CHAPTER 7: BREAKING DOWN THE BARRIERS – SHATTERING LIMITS

> **Bringing the first six chapters to life with real-world examples of what happened, what the outcomes were, what was learned, etc.**

OK, we are going in. Hold on to your hats, people, as it is time to bring some of the barriers to life and provide real-world examples of when these barriers have been faced, what happened, what the outcome was, and what was learned. Not all stories are going to result in breaking through the barriers – some may include running into the barrier at full speed and being stopped in your tracks. Regardless of the outcome, there is a lesson to learn from them all. We started this book by discussing what authenticity is and the various barriers that exist, and this chapter will focus on the general barriers to authenticity, while the next chapter will focus on those specific barriers that exist for women.

For this chapter, the approach will be to go through each of the various barriers with an example of what can happen, the good and the bad, along with what I have tried and tested in the past. And, of course, there will be some useful hints and tips of ways to either climb over the barrier or knock that bad boy down!

## Fear of rejection

There are times in your career where you will be asked to attend an event, a community or a workshop where you do not know everyone. It can be daunting, especially those first

10 to 15 minutes where everyone has to introduce themselves. One of my worst nightmares in these sessions is when we have to share "one fun fact" or "something that you can't find on LinkedIn". This is because I like to keep my work and private lives separate, so typically I am an open book on LinkedIn for information that is appropriate for the professional world.

I was invited to be part of a Women in Leadership movement during one of my previous roles. I was the only woman from the technology function to be invited, as it was a new initiative, and I was excited to be part of it. This was especially important to me as I had grown up in a house with a true feminist for a mum who championed equality and equity for women (and everyone) and I am keen to do the same. I was not sure who would be part of the group, but as it was organised from within the company, I would know everyone there at least by name if not through interactions at work.

As I have just said, the introductions part of the meeting is not something I enjoy. I find that it is easier in a room filled with people I have never met before, but when I do know the people, my heart starts pounding that little more as I wait for my turn. This links to my introverted nature, which I have learned over the years to overcome (or as much as possible – sometimes it is good to feel those nerves and the pounding of your heart), along with a lifelong shyness, especially in social situations (if you know me through work and are struggling to match this with my workplace Sophie persona, remember that I have had years of practice at building that persona). I think something that always haunts me about the introductions is that everyone else seems to say cool things and I feel out of place, or unsure of what to say. And then there is the whole thing of "do I want to go first and risk setting the wrong tone", "do I want to go last and risk not being able to live up to the standard set by everyone else?". Yes, I know this sounds a lot like thoughts associated with imposter syndrome, and you would be right.

For the first meeting of the leadership group, we were gathered around a table in the massive boardroom. I knew I wanted to talk about the importance of authenticity to me, and I was looking for support in leadership to create a psychologically safe environment for all colleagues to be their authentic selves. I thought that perhaps I could open the lid of the authenticity box a bit more than usual. I cannot remember if I went first or not, but I definitely was one of the first people to do their mini profile/introduction. The people before me were relatively frank and open, which gave me the confidence to say what I wanted to say rather than muting my authenticity to what I felt was a more acceptable level.

I spoke briefly about who I am, my motives for being part of the group and geared up to say something about being a woman in tech, the challenges I have faced both professionally and personally and then I let them have it.

Before I continue, I want to share that I am on my best behaviour while writing this book, but out in the real world, there are times when I swear like it is punctuation. It is neither something I am proud of, nor ashamed of. It is part of who I am and, having grown up on the 'wrong side' of town, I was swearing from about eight years old. My mother would not tolerate bad language and taught me to be respectful of others – if she caught me swearing, I would be in a heap of trouble ("crap" was considered a swear word in our house), so I learned from an early age when it is appropriate to use colourful language and when it is not.

I told the meeting participants: "I personally don't care about where someone is from, what their background is, what their sexual orientation is, what their beliefs are, or anything like that. In my opinion, there are two types of people in the world – you're either an arsehole or you're not."

As I spoke, some of the people around the table appeared to be shocked and disgusted at my use of language. I immediately felt like I had dialled up the authenticity too much, that I had said something wrong, that perhaps this was not the group for me and that I would not fit in. I wrapped up what I was saying quickly because I went from feeling empowered to feeling like the Sophie they had just been introduced to was not going to fit the mould of what they were trying to create.

What happened next? Well, I dialled down the amount of 'Sophie' I shared with the group. The negative reaction did not come from the whole group. For the ones who did react, it could have been a momentary thing as people often do not expect me to swear when they look at me. It could have been a perceived reaction and that due to situations in the past, I was being overly sensitive to the vibes in the room. I did not ask if what I had said shocked them, so I do not really know. But I do know how I felt. I felt that it was too much for that group of individuals for me to be my true self so I reined it back in.

It is fair to say that I did not feel out-and-out rejection from all the people present in that meeting, but I also left the room knowing that I did not and would not fit into the wider group. This was not something new, but it was a source of disappointment.

From a lessons-learned perspective, it has not changed the approach I take when introducing myself to others. Of course, I am going to be conscious of the audience, the surroundings and a variety of other factors to ensure I am professional in my delivery, however, my stance on being myself has not changed.

I do not go to work to make friends. Making friends at work is a bonus.

It is important to distinguish between getting on with people and building professional working relationships from truly being friends. I go to work to perform a role, to deliver to clients and to progress both the organisation and myself to mutually successful outcomes that deliver value. This is a key foundation to my approach in the workplace. And alongside it, I make no apology for being myself and authentic. I do recognise that it is not possible for everyone to be friends and get on – this is a fact of life – and with those whom I may not mesh as well with, I will still be polite, friendly and professional in my interactions with them. Like I have said at various places throughout this book, I believe in leading with empathy and being kind. Anything outside of this is not who I am, regardless of whether I am friends with someone or not.

## Social conditioning, cultural or societal pressures and expectations

We live in a world where we learn the norms and what is considered acceptable in society from an early age. These norms could be considered social conditioning, which can be positive but can also be detrimental. We have spoken about these when discussing what authenticity is and the barriers to it. In the workplace, I have encountered a variety of examples of social conditioning that have posed a challenge or stunted the ability of people to be their authentic selves.

## 7: Breaking down the barriers – Shattering limits

One of the most important examples in the workplace relates to the deference we are generally taught to have when it comes to respecting your elders and when respecting the hierarchy in an organisation. Before I walk through a specific scenario to illustrate this point, it is appropriate to state that I believe in leading with empathy, treating others with kindness and respect as a general rule, regardless of a person's position in the workplace or life, age or any other characteristic. That being said, I also firmly believe in the need for critical thinking, to be curious and to question the status quo.

Let me ask you a question.

How many times have you been told to deliver a piece of work because someone of authority in the organisation wants it but what they are asking for is either nonsensical, superfluous or downright stupid?

I suspect the answer to this question is: "More times than I'd like to remember."

Here is a follow-up question.

How many times have you or your colleagues completed the request, even though you knew it was not a valuable activity to complete, without asking a question?

I suspect the answer to this question is also: "More times than I'd like to remember."

There will be people in your organisation who are "yes" people, who will never question what they have been asked to do, purely deferring to the status of the requestor ("they're the boss", "this is above my paygrade to question", "I do not want to put my head above the parapet", etc.), regardless of what is being asked. Each to their own; it is their choice to do so.

However, this is not the path I personally follow – it does not align with who I am as a person to blindly agree to do something without understanding the rationale and the 'why'. As my experience in the working world has grown, I have come to the realisation that I have been employed as a subject matter expert (SME) to fulfil a role in an organisation. As an SME, it is important that I support the company I work for by providing advice, guidance and introducing solid frameworks, approaches, etc. Part of my role is to ask pertinent questions, advise of any potential risks and ensure that the people in positions of authority have as much information as possible to help them make informed decisions.

Allow me to share with you the approach I would typically follow in the circumstance where someone of authority in the organisation asks me to do something that does not make sense or seems like an ineffective use of time.

**Scenario:**

- A senior leader has asked me to prepare a report providing details of current service status, the strategies to manage high-profile incidents, what the three-year plan for managing key vendors is, along with an estimation of the cost of high-priority, business impacting incidents (typically referred to as P1 and P2 incidents in the technology world).

**Background and problem areas:**

- Regular reporting for major incidents and service status is completed both weekly and monthly – both of which are shared with senior leadership across the organisation.

- There is a third-party-supplier risk and governance forum that discusses operational issues as well as including the longer-term plans for driving effective relationships with suppliers.
- The IT strategy has been shared with the senior leadership team, which includes third- party management strategies.
- The cost per incident is gauged from an impacted-revenue perspective.
- There are multiple factors to consider when determining the cost per incident from a technology-function perspective, some of which will be incredibly difficult to estimate due to a lack of baselined salaries, time spent per incident, the complexity of each major incident, the cost of the technology and additional third-party costs, etc.
- There is already a lengthy list of items on my 'to do' list, many of which already originated from the senior leadership team.

## The approach:

- Receive the request and diligently make notes of what is required.
- Ask questions, but in a respectful and curious way, not bombarding the person but approaching them in a "I am seeking to gain insight and understanding" way:
  - Ask general questions about the task, such as:

- When is it needed by?
- Who needs it?
- What format should it take?
- What level of detail is required?
- Does it need to go through to the CIO to review and send out? Or am I sending it directly to the stakeholders who want it?
- Is this a one-off request? Or does this need to be a regular requirement?

o Ask specific questions about the task, probing the rationale such as:
  - Is there a specific reason why the report is needed now?
  - Are there any data concerns or compliance reasons why the information is needed?
  - Where does this report fit in with the monthly reporting that is already available to the senior leadership team?
  - How does this fit in with the existing strategy and information available?
  - Are there any concerns referring to existing strategies and processes that could be used to ensure the timeliest collation of the information?

- In all the questioning, I would be using my body language to show I have listened, making notes and replaying some of the answers to show that I have understood what is being asked of me.

- Now it is time to set expectations by talking about prioritisation and how this piece of work fits into other priorities and deliverables. To do this, your approach will likely differ depending on who you are speaking to.
  - If it is your boss, the question would be: "Given all the other priorities I'm working on, how does this fit in from your perspective because if this is the number 1 priority, other deliverables such as xxxx and xxxx will need to be pushed back?"
  - If it is not your boss, I would typically say something along the lines of: "OK, thank you for the information. I will go back to the team and check in with <line manager's name> to advise of the prioritisation and to set expectations on other deliverables I am currently working on."
- The purpose of bringing up the prioritisation is to show the person that you acknowledge and understand what is being asked of you, and who the request is for, while also maintaining that the position of this request is likely to have a butterfly effect on the other things you are working on.
- To further set expectations, I would also mention there being some challenges you will face to pull together the information as well as needing an element of collaboration from other areas of the business, such as the payroll/HR team to obtain salary benchmarking, AND that some of the information will need to be a best guess or guesstimate due to variables associated.

Through the course of the interaction, I am focusing on being respectful to the person of authority while also asking the appropriate questions to build an understanding of the 'why'.[30] I am conscious that I want to live within the boundaries of respect and hierarchy while not agreeing to an onerous piece of work that will be time-consuming to the cost of my other deliverables.

This is just one type of social conditioning.

Another example is in relation to constant negative feedback about the communications sent out when there is a major incident and a technology service is not working.

**This is a true story.**

The usual major-incident process kicks into place and communications (comms) need to be sent to all stakeholders to let them know what is happening. (This is often a task of the service desk team if you do not have a dedicated incident management team.) The service desk team sends comms out and receives feedback from multiple sources along the lines of:

- There is too much detail;
- There is not enough detail;
- You missed key information;
- You need to remove technical terms;

---

[30] There are, of course, times where you do just have to do as the boss wants you to. There may be information you are not privy to that would provide context of why you are being asked to do something. It is an area where you need to consider the situation and how far you are prepared to push your curiosity to understand the purpose of what you are being asked to do. There is no hard and fast rule to how to approach this – it comes down to experience and knowing your stakeholders.

- You need to include technical terms;
- Your use of language was not suitable for a wider business audience; and
- Your use of language was not suitable for those whose native language is not English.

This list could go on and on, but you get the idea that the feedback in this case was not positive, consistent or encouraging.

Now, fast forward six months, where there have been multiple major incidents and the feedback on the comms has been consistently inconsistent and utterly unhelpful. What you now have is a service desk team that has been conditioned to receive negative feedback about any communications it sends out during a major incident. And a reluctance or reticence from the service desk analysts to be the sacrificial lamb who needs to send the next comms, to be the one taking the brunt of the criticism.

The way to address this was through education, affirmation and building confidence within the service desk team to be resilient to the stream of negative feedback, learning how to filter the useful feedback from the rest of it.

A workshop was set up with the service desk team to discuss the feedback they had received, to create a space where they could openly talk about how it made them feel and walk through any concerns they had about sending comms in the future. It was a psychologically safe space for them to vent their opinions and thoughts without fear of repercussion. We went through a variety of scenarios; what was the best language to use; what were good examples of previous comms and ones that needed to be improved upon. The session was also an opportunity for the team members to set their standards of how to approach scenarios with a solid structure for sending major-incident comms going forwards. Once set, the standards could then be communicated to the wider technology leadership team to set their expectations and introduce an appropriate escalation process for them to provide feedback if needed.

In essence, the workshop's intention (while also being to define the standards and drive consistency for sending comms out) was to empower the team and break down some of the conditioning that had been introduced.

## Perfectionism and lack of vulnerability

### *Perfectionism*

As a general rule, people want to do a good job and deliver their work to a good/high standard. For some, delivering anything less than what is considered 'perfect' is a cause of anxiety or concern about what that would mean to their professional reputation.

When I was younger, I would refer to myself as a perfectionist and the little things would irritate me if they were not quite right. I would say things to myself like:

- "I need to do this piece of work to the highest quality, even though I don't have the information I need or there are gaps."
- "I don't want to miss the deadline."
- "I'm worried about what will happen if I don't get this spot on, even though I can only know what I know."

As I have aged, I have realised that perfection is an ideal, not a reality. It is like professionalism as an ideal – it will differ from person to person as to what it means. There may be similarities between people's definition of professionalism but there will be nuances and differences based on experience, upbringing and a whole range of influencing factors. The same can be said of what 'perfect' means to each person.

> **Tip:**
>
> **Perfection is an ideal, not a reality.**

Here is an example:

I am a visual person. I like reports and presentations to not only have good content, but I also want them to be aesthetically pleasing. In every organisation I have worked in, I follow the branding guidelines for any documents I produce to ensure they are on point and in keeping with the company's brand. When I have been in an organisation for a length of time, I can typically spot when the colours being used in a presentation are not the right branding colours, even when they are similar. In one role, my team used to tweak the design to see if I would spot the use of the wrong font or colour, and they used to tease me when I would spot them each time.

This may sound silly as surely it is the content that matters? However, I believe that the visual representation of information is part of your professional image and profile, which can impact your reputation. A way to illustrate this further is to talk about your CV. If you are applying for a role that requires you to engage with senior leadership, to write reports and present information yet your CV is poorly formatted, wordy and looks like a visual assault on the senses, this says something about you. Your CV is like your calling card. How you present yourself in it says something about you.

Going back to the idea of perfection, it is important to remember that it is not possible to be perfect. Whatever ideals you may have or feel others have about you, they are not necessarily something that you can live up to or want to live up to. With regards to the people around you, part of the question here is, do you want to live up to those ideals? Does that align with your values? To fit a mould of 'perfection' may require you to try to be something you are not and that is the opposite of authenticity.

### Lack of vulnerability

Often combined with perfectionism is a lack of vulnerability and not wanting to look anything less than perfect. Essentially, forgetting the basic principle that as humans we are all flawed and there is no such thing 'perfect'.

Have you ever kept working on a report or piece of work after it is finished to make last-minute tweaks, to get it 'just so' and then after you have sent it, checked it again and realised that something was not 100% perfect in it or that there was a slight mistake? What have you done when that has happened? Have you openly admitted that there was a mistake or have you sent an email saying something like "apologies, this is the right version, the other one was a draft"?

I personally have done both at various times in my career, but these days I am more likely to do the first one and openly say I have made a mistake, even as a consultant. Of course, I want to make sure I am presenting myself in the best light, but at the same time I see the benefit of showing that I am human – sharing a level of vulnerability with the people that I am working with.

The thing with being vulnerable in the workplace is that it does not mean that you need to bare your soul to your colleagues and talk deep-seated emotions – not at all. Vulnerability is also admitting that you are capable of not being perfect and that is OK.

Personally, I put a lot more faith in a leader who is able to admit mistakes and wrongdoing than one who maintains an appearance of perfection and never admits that sometimes they do things wrong.

**Lack of self-awareness and low self-esteem**

How do you know if you are self-aware? You could argue that you have absolutely no idea if you are or not, which could mean that you have a lack of self-awareness.

Let us spend a bit of time discovering things that you can do to build your self-awareness, which may also result in an increase in self-esteem through understanding yourself better.

**Understanding yourself through self-reflection**: ask yourself things like:

- What triggered me just now and why?
- Why did I react that way?
- Am I projecting something onto this situation?
- What are my intentions going into this situation and what does that mean?
- What were my motivations in this situation?

**Recognising your strengths and weaknesses**, although I like to call weaknesses 'development areas' instead as it has a more positive connotation. To put it bluntly, you need to cut through the bullshit. Be objective about who you are, with the aim of accepting yourself for all your positives and strengths as well as development areas. Invest time in understanding your flaws and things that you want to work on, and in building a personal-development plan. Building this plan could also include seeking support from a coach or mentor to help you on that journey (both coaching and mentoring are discussed in more detail later in the book).

### Tip:

**Weaknesses can be reframed so they're viewed as development areas rather than seeing them through a negative light.**

**Taking accountability and responsibility for yourself**, and your actions. If something goes wrong, it is important to understand the part you played. For example, if you end up in a conflict situation that escalates to raised voices and a heated conversation, it is important to understand the role you played in that conversation. What could you have done differently? Was there anything in your tone or use of words that could have incited the reaction from the other person? From the interaction, what are you accountable for? Sometimes situations occur unprovoked, but it is important to reflect and draw conclusions objectively.

This also applies the other way when things have gone well. Giving credit where it is due, including to yourself. There is nothing wrong with patting yourself on the back after a job well done. Self-awareness and objectivity lead to recognition of an achievement and not arrogance, potentially still seeking out opportunities to develop and improve.

**Be open to feedback**, even when it is not glowing. It is important to listen to feedback to see if there is anything you can learn or gain from the perspective of others. It is also important to take the feedback at face value and to listen, even if you do not agree with it. Again, this is key with positive feedback. Allowing yourself to have done a good job, taking the compliment, even when it makes you uncomfortable.

In the world of technology and providing services to a business, one of the phrases we use is about being only as good as the last major incident, where there is often a raft of feedback on what should have or could have happened. But this side of technology is a fraction of the time spent delivering valuable and effective services, and it is important to take time to see positive feedback. It is valuable to celebrate successes.

**Understanding how you affect others and any patterns that exist**. It is key that if you hurt someone, even if not on purpose, that you care about it and take the time to make it right, apologising for your actions (back to accountability and responsibility). If you have behaviours that become cyclical or relationship dynamics that are not healthy, you need to reflect and understand how they happen, identifying ways to address them (back to self-awareness).

An example here is procrastination. We all do it and I can be terribly guilty of it. I can get caught up in a TikTok doom scroll and before I know it, my lunch hour has gone. I have not had anything to eat and it is time to go back to work. But I need to get back into work with the right mindset and I have squandered my downtime watching funny cat videos. (This is a true story and happens more times than I like to admit.) Part of my self-awareness here is taking steps to limit the procrastination, ensuring that I am giving myself enough time to eat and do any chores I have put off by scrolling.

Another example is the use of language in meetings, specifically those meetings where some of the attendees present may not speak the same language as you. If you are someone who typically speaks quickly and have a broad accent, it may be difficult for the people in the meeting to follow what you are saying. Pause, take your time when speaking, allow people to catch up and process what you are saying. Check understanding and involve people in the conversation to make sure they do not feel overwhelmed. Make sure you leave plenty of time for the attendees to ask questions, or have the opportunity to feed back after the meeting.

**Maintaining your self-esteem takes work**. Unless you are incredibly lucky, your self-esteem can be like a rollercoaster with ups and downs throughout your life. Working on all the areas above will give you an insight into what makes you who you are. It should, if you are truly objective, highlight those areas where you excel and are facets of you to recognise, celebrate and be proud of. We will be speaking shortly about mental health, which self-esteem is linked to, but please know that your self-worth is determined by you and, while others may have an opinion, be your own compass direction.

### Toxic relationships/leadership/environments and the pressure to succeed

I have worked in a variety of organisations of different sizes, cultures, values and industries. In my career so far, I have also worked in more toxic environments that I would care to remember and had to manage being in some toxic relationships with leadership.

"Shut the fuck up!" a direct line manager once told me in a one-to-one meeting where I was voicing an opinion after being asked for it. The relationship with this manager was challenging because he came from an 'old school' IT background where IT should be seen and not heard. This view does not align with my vision of championing the technology department and its achievements (while also ensuring there is accountability when things go wrong at the hands of technology). Needless to say, this was an area of contention between me and my line manager. In addition to this, it was unclear if he had had a direct report like me before – female, opinionated and not afraid to voice my opinion.

When he told me to "shut the fuck up", I was taken back. I had not been raising my voice or dogged in my approach. He just did not like what I was saying and wanted to silence me. If you have read the previous chapters you will know by this point in the book that I have no qualms about standing up for myself and ensuring I am professional in doing so.

I wanted to reply with this: "Be careful. I may tell *you* to shut the fuck up if you keep going down this road." Instead, I combined my words with strong body language – standing tall, shoulders back, appearing relaxed but firm to ensure my response came across as professional and not crossing any lines or perpetuating the same or similar behaviour in return. I said: "You cannot talk to me like that. I am not someone you can dominate. I will not be silent because you don't like what I've said. And I'll use your own words back at you: swear at me, I'll swear at you – without appearing crass. And I'll do all this without raising my voice or breaking a sweat."

This same person also liked to talk over me in meetings in front of my peers and others, which initially resulted in others trying to do the same. I cannot speak for the male readers here, but to my female readers, you will have been in this situation where someone talks over you in a meeting, trying to dominate, to belittle or lessen your position.

The younger version of me would wait patiently for the person to make their point, and then I would chime in again, trying to get my thoughts across. However, I learned an approach that is my favourite thing to do when being talked over. I use the method of repeating myself in a calm, professional manner, like a broken record repeating the same thing but in a positive, assertive manner:

- "If you'd just let me finish" <pause>
- "If you'd just let me finish" <pause>
- A little louder: "If you'd just let me finish" <pause>
- Finally, loudly (but not shouting), delivered slowly: "If you'd just let me finish" combined with direct eye contact.

> **Tip:**
> Trying the broken record method when being spoken over, is an assertive and professional approach to highlight poor etiquette/behaviour without inciting conflict.

### *Having my authenticity questioned*

It was time for me to level up in my career. Or at least ensure that the senior leadership team was aware that I was setting my sights on career progression to become a CIO or equivalent. I had been the head of service management for three years and regularly deputised for my boss, the existing CIO, on a regular basis – although without the official title of 'deputy'. I was well respected in my peer group, throughout the technology function and the wider business. While I am not someone who has a specific career trajectory in mind, I am ambitious and keen to progress – ultimately expanding my skills, knowledge and expertise to continually improve and grow.

My boss was leaving the organisation, leaving the CIO role vacant. Now let me be clear – I had no delusions of grandeur and did not assume to be the successful candidate, but I did think it was important for me to throw my hat in the ring, to raise my profile with the C-suite senior leadership team. It was important to show to the big bosses that they had an internal candidate who was looking to expand their skillset and responsibilities in a way that would benefit both the company and the candidate.

I also wanted to make sure that I did not waste anyone's time by applying for the role, so I reached out to the managing director (MD), asking if he could spare ten minutes for me to speak to him. The conversation was positive, and I left hearing the words "you're a viable candidate, yes". After this conversation, I was no longer concerned about wasting anyone's time by applying to be the new CIO.

Having never applied for a C-suite role before, I did not really know what to expect from the recruitment process, but I suspected it would be a lot more in-depth and vigorous than the ones I had been involved in before. I was right. An external headhunting company did an initial call to see who you were and whether you were a good fit based on the requirements given to them. Then there was a questionnaire to complete, where you needed to respond to a variety of questions about who you were, what your values were, what your experience had been in certain areas, how your previous experience could contribute to the success of the role and organisation, and so on. Depending on your responses and the initial conversation with the head-hunter, you would then get through to the first round of interviews with members of the C-suite.

I completed the questionnaire to the best of my ability. Where there were gaps in my experience, I flagged them while including reference to my knowledge of the organisation, the technology function, where it was headed and my vision to support its journey. I spoke about my stakeholder-management style, which is firm and forthright, while being polite and friendly. Having been bullied from an early age, I know how important it is to treat others with empathy and kindness, even in conflict situations. I also understand the importance of balancing this with the need to be firm, set boundaries and understand that being a leader does not always mean being liked.

I was known in the office as someone who was true to their values and would be fair but firm when things needed to be addressed. If you have ever dealt with a major incident where human error is the root cause, you will know this is important. Having a psychologically safe environment is key for any workforce, in that allowing people to fail is OK. It is also vital to ensure the risks associated with human error are minimised when it comes to delivering technology-based services (especially in some industries where the tech services failing could impact peoples' lives). I had been given the nickname 'smiling assassin' in the past – something that did not necessarily stem from a positive foundation, but I actually like the nickname. To me, it means delivering bad news with the audience in mind. To go in with the mindset of "I need to tell you that something has gone wrong" and the attitude of "I understand how this will impact you, but we will rectify it and make it better to minimise the effect the issue will have on you".

The initial conversation with the head-hunter went well. They were very clear that I was in a pool of candidates with far more experience than me, but the feedback was that it was likely I would be put through to the interview stage with the big bosses.

Four weeks went by and I had not heard anything about the next stage of interviews or whether I had been put through. I contacted the MD to ask if there were any updates and was invited to a meeting with him to discuss my application. I had not heard anything from the head-hunter either, so I knew this was not an interview but hopefully I would get some insight into the recruitment process and the next steps, if there were any for me.

I told my boss about the meeting and his words of advice were "make sure you're on time as the MD does not like people being late". As someone who leaves 30 minutes before a doctor's appointment, when the surgery is a five-minute drive, I had no intention of being late but thanked my boss for the advice and made sure I was there with plenty of time to spare.

I got to the meeting room five minutes early (I did not want to look too keen) and walked past the MD chatting to some people on my way. I did not want to interrupt him, so just went straight to the meeting room and sat down.

The MD came in five minutes after the start time, and as he was walking into the room, he said, "Has anyone told you that you haven't got the job?"

There was no "hello" or other greeting. He just casually strolled in, did not even sit down, barely looked at me, and that was his opening line.

Now, as much as I am true to my values, there is a line where I am not going to just accept such a lack of civility and manners from people.

My smile dropped slightly, to ensure my message was going to be received as I intended it (firm, shocked but still polite). I looked directly at him to make eye contact and my response was: "Yes, you've just told me."

I think this may have jolted him into realising how thoughtless and, quite frankly, rude he was, as he sat down for us to have a conversation about the application as a whole.

What followed was possibly one of the most disappointing conversations I have ever had, not because I did not get the role but because of how the message was delivered. This was someone who I had thought highly of as a strong and inspiring leader, and their approach to delivering bad news to one of their team was shocking. I would like to say that the initial bombshell was the only one in the meeting, but sadly it was not.

When talking about my application and in particular the responses I had given about how I manage stakeholders (being forthright and firm while being polite), he said, "It's all a question of your authenticity." He went on to explain that he had asked one person about me (yes, just one person), who could not vouch that how I had described my approach was accurate. He also said that another area that did not make me a viable candidate was that I did not get to the point or summarise the actions or key focus areas when communicating with others.

To say that I was gobsmacked at both what he said and how he said it, is an understatement.

I responded in the politest way possible, conscious that this was the head of the company, and the decision had already been made. But I wanted to challenge this view of my character, so I expressed that I had never had anyone question my authenticity before and I was surprised that this was the assessment of me.

I provided some context of my leadership style and leading with empathy, and perhaps that my communication style during conflict or difficult situations differs from others. To address the perception that I do not get to the point, I spoke about the monthly board report I wrote for the existing CIO, which was written to suit the C-suite audience, was succinct, with clear calls to action. The response I received was: "There's more to being a CIO than writing presentations."

It was at this point I knew that the conversation was not about letting me down gently or providing advice and guidance to support my development. It was a conversation where the MD had to deliver bad news and get something off the to-do list, but in doing so, he had not only questioned my authenticity but also questioned my ability to operate at a senior level after having previously told me I was a viable candidate (his words, not mine).

I was extremely upset, but I was not going to drop the professional persona to let that show. I went back to my desk and carried on with my day. I needed to process what had been said to me, and how it had been communicated.

I felt that I needed to be careful about how I spoke about what was said and who with, because at the end of the day, it was the big boss who had behaved poorly. I did not want to impact how others perceived him. I spoke to trusted members of my peer group who I knew would be completely honest if they thought what was said was an accurate reflection of how I appear in the office, and whether it was right for my authenticity to have been questioned. To my relief, they agreed that my assessment of how I approach conflict and manage stakeholders was correct and authentic.

### *The takeaway*

It is not always going to go to plan.

There are times when your jokes, your humour, your personality will not mesh well with those around you. I am not ashamed to confess that I have not had a perfect, drama-free journey to being my authentic self. The story I have just told is testament to the fact that where I thought I was being truly authentic, there was a perception from someone else that I was not.

A few months after this event, I had the opportunity to take another role in the organisation or to leave and work elsewhere. I chose to leave for a variety of reasons. One of the key contributors to my decision was this interaction with the MD. Not everyone finds themselves in the situation where they can leave a toxic environment. I was 'lucky' in some senses of the word, and chose to remove myself from an environment that formed a barrier to authenticity, where my authenticity was openly questioned, without just cause.

It is important that you accept imperfection in yourself and others. It is also important to know when it is OK to walk away.

Accept that sometimes…shit happens.

> **Tip:**
>
> **Remember it is not always going to go to plan. You may need to adapt; course correct and learn along the way.**

## Mental-health challenges

I wish that there was a way to make things better quickly when people are struggling with their mental health, but unfortunately this just is not the case. There is no quick fix, nor a hard and fast rule that will help you overcome any mental-health challenges you have.

I am not a counsellor, nor do I have a background in therapy, but I have experienced my own challenges with mental health, which have at times been a barrier to me being authentic at work. To provide you with some context here, I am going to tell you a story about my time during the COVID-19 pandemic.

In March 2020, along with the rest of the United Kingdom, the country went into a lockdown in an attempt to prevent the spread of coronavirus. I was single at the time and living alone with my two daughters, who were both in high school. We all found it bizarre at first but soon the isolation from others began to weigh heavily on everyone in the house. The initial announcement citing the rules of lockdown were updated within 24 hours, so that my children could still maintain contact with their father, which meant that every other weekend, the girls would go to stay with their dad – a semblance of the previous normal routine.

## 7: Breaking down the barriers – Shattering limits

Before lockdown, those weekends when my children were away were ones filled with hiking, walking, travelling and exploring – usually by myself as I thoroughly enjoy my own company. My mini adventures were a way for me to feel free of the responsibilities of everyday life, even if only for a few hours, and just enjoy the time being Sophie. But during lockdown, something happened to me and no matter what I did, I could not escape the burden of responsibility, I could not find anything close to a semblance of peace. It constantly felt like I was in a room that was shrinking, and I could not find my way out.

I went on daily walks locally – pushing my body as far as I could to wear myself out. Not small walks, I am talking six-to-eight-mile walks in the Yorkshire countryside that is minutes from my front doorstep. For those of your who are not familiar with what Yorkshire and the north of England is like, it is very hilly with deep valleys and steep surrounding hills. It is beautiful. It is also physically challenging in terms of walks and cycle routes. I was physically fit, but I was putting my body under a lot of pressure, which has had its repercussions, which is a whole other story. While I would have brief moments of relief when out walking, they were short-lived because every step I took meant I was heading back home to the same four walls.

My interaction with other humans went from speaking regularly to people face to face to that being a rarity and a treat. I would seldom see anyone when I went out for a walk and if there were others out and about, we would keep a significant distance from each other to abide by the rules and to stay safe. Often crossing the road from others to maintain a suitable and safe distance. When my children were at home, I would, of course, have the opportunity to speak to them, but they were going through their own struggles with the isolation as well as being teenagers, who were in the phase of their childhood where they stayed in their room a lot of the time.

It got to the point where going to the supermarket was the highlight of my week. Queuing outside until it was my turn to go in, walk round the shop and then go through the checkout – this was my only in-person interaction with anyone other than my daughters. And when it was a weekend, and my girls were with their dad, it was THE ONLY CONTACT WITH ANOTHER HUMAN in a 48-hour period.

I am an introvert, and I love my own company. I often find myself with a depleted battery when it comes to social events and after busy days at work, where I have needed to engage heavily with others. The reverse became true during lockdown – the continued isolation and lack of interaction with my fellow humans became something I craved to have back. The time spent going through the checkout at the supermarket each week was my opportunity to talk to someone else, and those conversations were pretty much the same each week – mundane and with no real substance. But regardless of how exciting the conversation was, it was still an opportunity to interact with another human. The hole that had been created by the isolation was temporarily filled in that small, seemingly meaningless, interaction.

The cycle became oppressive, and I could feel the weight of depression on my shoulders, making everyday life during this time even harder than it already was, while trying to survive the lockdowns.

At work, however, I felt like I needed to put on a 'brave face' and set an example for my team and colleagues, offering support and encouragement during a time everyone found difficult. My role as a senior leader needed me to lead by example, to maintain the status quo while continuing to deliver for the business. During working hours, I would shove how I was feeling to one side. I would slap a smile on my face and display the mask of someone who has it all under control. Someone who was not struggling with depression and who could be a tower of strength for those around her.

People do mask to a degree, but the extent to which I was masking deviated from who I usually am. Typically at work, I would share how I feel about things and some of my home life to set expectations for those around me if there was a lot going on that may see a slight change in behaviour on my part. During the period of time around the various lockdowns, I did not do this. I kept quiet and hid how I was feeling.

Time passed and slowly the dark place I had found myself in had a light at the end of the tunnel. My mental health improved over time, and I found myself being ready to talk about how I felt and what I had experienced.

As one of the senior leadership team at the company I was working at, I regularly spoke at town hall meetings and events about a variety of topics. Typically, it would have had a technology or service management focus, but there was one town hall scheduled during mental-health-awareness month, so I tabled the idea of talking about mental-health issues and offered to lead the charge and talk about my own mental health.

The session I delivered was all about how hard I had found the isolation of lockdown, how hard I had found going from being in the office five days a week to zero days a week. The times where I would go through a whole day without interacting with another human, and importantly, how that made me feel. The town hall was for my technology and cyber security colleagues, roughly 120 people, with an estimated 80/20 split between men and women. After the session, I had several colleagues, mostly men, message me to say how much they appreciated someone in a leadership role talking about mental health and finding it hard.

The moral of the story here is that sometimes it is OK for poor mental health to be a barrier to being truly authentic. Sometimes, all you can do is survive and get through the day. I recognise now that same barrier in similar situations, but the important part is that I shared my journey and what happened, creating a psychologically safe space for colleagues to share similar experiences.

Below are some of the things you can do to process any mental-health challenges you are facing, and there are some useful links in the appendix, too.

- Acknowledge how and what you are feeling – holding it in can make it worse.
- Talk to someone – a friend, a counsellor, a doctor – you are not alone.
- Get some fresh air and vitamin D – sometimes going for a walk helps gain perspective.
- Write it down – use a journal or equivalent to get the thoughts out.
- When the thoughts go to a negative space, challenge them – remember what we said earlier about reframing for a different perspective and about being kind to yourself.

- Introduce a routine, even a small one – take it step by step in bite-sized chunks and introduce simple rituals like a walk, a morning coffee, doing a crossword, etc.
- Try to limit potentially toxic inputs – social media or doom-scrolling, overstimulation, etc.
- Try to find some calm or mindfulness – deep breathing, yoga or meditation.
- Accept that it may be a bumpy road to recovery – the path to healing is rarely linear; it is OK to have bad days and to cry.
- Ask for professional help if it becomes overwhelming – I have been speaking to a counsellor for the last 12 months because I no longer wanted to carry the weight of the past with me everywhere I went. I had tried going it alone and recognised I needed support from a professional to work through the past.

# CHAPTER 8: BREAKING DOWN THE BARRIERS – DEFYING THE NORM

> Continuing to bring the earlier chapters to life with real-world examples of what happened, what the outcomes were, what was learned, etc.

As with the previous chapter, we are going back to the beginning of the book and Chapter 3, where we discussed what the barriers to authenticity are for women in the workplace. We will use the same headers as discussed in Chapter 3, where we will have a real-life story of how this barrier can play itself out in the workplace, or in life generally, along with advice and tips on how to break that barrier down.

## Gender bias and stereotyping

We will start with a story. Remember: if you have read the "About the Author" section, you will know that I was bullied at school, so you will understand why I am not a fan of confrontation, and it has taken years to find the courage and delivery approach to manage confrontational situations. However, I will stand up for myself when I feel it is a battle worth fighting. Although, when I stand up for myself, it will be in a calm, collected and measured way to ensure my message is clear. I want my intentions and thoughts to be known, understood and for the people I am speaking with to understand their next steps or actions and to take accountability for themselves.

For the scenario in question, I had only been in the company for about six months, and I was sitting at my desk area with my line manager and other colleagues. The other desks in the row were occupied by other members of the technology team. Behind me, the head of technology had a single desk with a table next to it where small meetings took place. I used to love this desk arrangement because there would be all sorts of people stopping by throughout the day to have conversations with my manager and the head of technology. It was a great opportunity to meet new people.

It was close to the end of the working day and one of the IT managers from another office had come by to say farewell to the managers in my area. I was working at my desk and was not a part of the conversation going on behind me. I had already discovered that this particular individual seemed to have a tendency to focus on the male members of the team, unless there was some menial admin task to be done. In these scenarios, he had spoken to one of the women in the team. "Each their own" is one of my mottos, and I would generally ignore the behaviour.

Partway through the conversation behind me, I heard the visiting manager talk about needing to get a taxi to the train station, then he said loudly, "Sophie, book me a taxi to the train station!" It took me a couple of seconds to realise that this was not a joke. The person had not turned around to ensure they had my attention; they just barked the order for me to book them a taxi.

There were a plethora of emotions and thoughts that ran through me in that moment. One of which was pure rage along with a giant slab of shock. Here are some of the questions that went through my head:

- Who are you to bark orders at me?

- Are you incapable of picking up the phone and doing it yourself?
- Why are you asking me and not the people you are actually having a conversation with?
- Are you asking me because I am a woman?
- Do you lack the basic decency of looking at me when talking to me?
- Manners obviously cost too much for this person.
- Would it have been that difficult to say "please"?

Bear in mind that I had not been in the role for too long and was still unsure of how to manage these sorts of situations. OK, I had seen male colleagues in similar situations where they are asked to complete a task that was not part of their role responsibilities. However, I had not witnessed a male colleague being asked to keep the meeting minutes in a meeting, book a taxi, or perform stereotypically "female" tasks. The response from my male colleagues in these circumstances was typically a "No" or a firm response that clearly indicated they were not going to complete the task, but I did not know if it was possible for me to respond in a similar manner without there being some form of repercussion. I did not feel that I had had enough time in the role for these people to respond positively to my natural instincts on how to respond to the visiting manager.

So, I gritted my teeth and said slowly said "OK", drawing it out and in a tone that I hope expressed the disappointment and disgust at how I had been spoken to. The visiting manager did not respond with a "thank you" or acknowledging my existence, he just carried on talking to the managers behind me. I do not think that the tone of my response was lost on my line manager or the head of technology, but the visiting manager seemed oblivious.

I aggressively picked up the telephone and had a polite and friendly conversation with the staff on reception, asking them to arrange a taxi for the visiting manager and thanked them for their help. After hanging up the telephone and resting the handset back in the cradle slightly more firmly than normal, I turned to the group behind me and said, "<visiting manager's name>, your taxi has been booked."

You would think here there would have been a form of acknowledgement or a "thank you", but no, sadly not. He did not pause in the conversation he was having. He did not turn to look at me.

To say I was furious at this point would be an understatement. I was not just cross at the whole interaction (although to use the word 'interaction' implies there was some form of two-way communication when there was not), but I was also cross that MY direct managers had not said anything or made a comment (looking back now, the lack of response could well have been that I was one of the few women in the department and this kind of behaviour was not encountered regularly).

The visiting manager left the office shortly after this and I was still fuming. I was shocked that someone had behaved like that towards me and even more furious that it was taken as acceptable behaviour. I was the only woman in the team, and I was conscious of how all the men joked and laughed together. I also joked and laughed with the team. I had figured out early on in life how to use humour to fit into a group that I did not necessarily fully identify with.

I knew that I needed to say something to my manager and his boss. I did not want it to be a confrontation, and I also did not want it to be delivered in a jokey way, which had typically been my approach to date in this role. I needed to find the balance of controlling my rage with delivering a very clear, professionally expressed response to the situation. Just before I packed up for the day, I decided to ask my managers what they thought of the interaction and to set the expectation that if the same situation arose, that I expected them to call out the bad behaviour and support me (or any woman in the same situation).

I turned to my manager and the big boss and said:

"I'm not happy with how <visiting manager's name> spoke to me before. It was rude, it was borderline sexist and I'm no one's admin bitch. He did not even have the decency to turn around and speak to me face to face to address me, nor did he say 'please' or 'thank you'. If he ever does that to me again, I don't care what his position in the company is, I will be telling him to pick up the fucking phone and do it himself."

OK, so this was not necessarily hitting the fully professional mark that I had intended, but the whole situation had pissed me off and I needed to express myself when talking to the bosses about it. I did, however, deliver the message in a way that left no room for interpretation and clearly defined my boundaries with colleagues, especially sexist male colleagues.

I do not recall the bosses' exact responses, but I do recall them being slightly taken back. They had not seen this side of me before – only the polite, friendly and amenable-to-everything Sophie. I do remember them being supportive, however, and can say that the same situation did not occur again.

Bringing this back to breaking down barriers and being authentic, what is it that you can learn from this story?

To put it simply, it is about:

- Setting boundaries;
- Having the confidence to call out bad behaviour;
- Not being afraid to voice your opinion;
- Choosing the appropriate time to deal with negative behaviour; and
- Being true to your values.

Before moving on, it is important to share that after this situation happened and I had spoken to the two managers, I found a different level of confidence to express myself and to call out bad behaviours openly when they happened. How I do this will depend on the situation, who is in the room and what my relationship with them is. Sometimes, I will still use humour to sound like I am teasing but with a clear message of "pack it in"; at other times, I will be direct and call it as I see it. Here are some examples:

**Table 3: Situations and Responses**

| Situation overstepping a boundary | Response using humour | Response to the point |
|---|---|---|
| Asking the only woman in the room to make the teas and coffees | "Is there something in your physical make-up that | "No, but while you're getting your own drink, |

| | stops you doing this for yourself?" | I'll have a glass of water, thanks." |
|---|---|---|
| Asking the only woman in the room to take the meeting minutes and notes | "Oh, I see, it's a 'woman's' job, is it? Men can't take meeting minutes?" | "I have an idea. Let's alternate the responsibility of minute-taking to all attendees." |
| "Can you fix it as well as the boys can?" | "Only if they hold my hand, but that might make it difficult for me to put your PC back together." | "Yes, of course. I taught them." |

You can also ask someone outright if their comment was meant to be "hurtful or helpful". This puts them in a position where they have to respond and explain themselves or stay quiet and look foolish.

## The pressure to conform

I have already said that I am not someone who likes confrontation. There are times where, from the outside, it may seem that I am more compliant and compromising than I actually am. This is because I fight the battles worth fighting and generally take a measured approach to conflict. There are times where I have felt pressure from leadership, peers or even members of my team to conform to a way of behaving that aligns with their narrative, their truth and their idea of how people should behave.

Let me give you an example that has hidden conflict in it, which I will point out afterwards.

I was on a conference call with ten of my peers and two of the C-suite leadership team for the technology- and programme-delivery functions. I do not remember the topic, but it was a workshop that needed engagement from everyone on the call, as well as having formal minutes and actions captured for traction, maintaining momentum and accountability.

The person who usually took minutes was not available (we will call them Mary for the purpose of this story), so I offered to step into their shoes for the meeting. It is worth making a point here that Mary's role in attending the meeting was purely to take minutes and they were the only attendee who did not have an active participatory role in the meeting. My role was a delegate, to support the conversation and to engage with all attendees to drive the meeting forward.

Before the meeting kicked off properly, I made a joke asking everyone to not speak too quickly and allow me time to capture the conversations and key actions. While I said it as a joke, it was actually my way of saying the following:

- I am part of the meeting too, so allow me time to be involved while capturing the notes.
- Do not talk over each other; be respectful.
- Let us work collaboratively to collectively ensure we have an accurate record of the meeting.

Everyone responded positively apart from one of the C-suite attendees, who pulled a face and said, "I don't see why that's necessary as Mary doesn't have an issue capturing the minutes and actions, so why would you?" The tone in which it was said was rude, dismissive, curt and patronising. I was shocked that someone of that level would speak like that to someone who was offering help and support to fill a gap, especially in a room of their peers. If they did not like my comments, they should have addressed me separately rather than in front of everyone in the meeting.

As soon as they had asked their rhetorical question, belittling me in front of my peer group, the meeting went silent. One of those awkward silences where I would typically use my humour to say something to lighten the moment and move the conversation on, but on this occasion, I was too shocked at how I had been spoken to, and no one else said anything either.

It felt like the silence lasted for an incredibly long time, but I collected myself, smiled politely and said "OK", and the meeting carried on. I captured the minutes, asking people to repeat themselves if I needed to and circulated them after the session with no corrections or issues with the notes and actions I had shared.

After the meeting, a number of people, including my line manager, who was the other C-suite individual on the call, told me they were shocked at how I had been spoken to. And yet, no one had said anything in the meeting or offered any support or backup.

When talking about it with my boss, I expressed my disappointment with how the situation had played out. Sadly, I was not surprised that no one had spoken out, because the C-suite individual who made the comment was notorious for their tactless, empathy-free and rude approach. I had heard rumours of a toxic culture growing in the function they headed up, however, I had not seen anyone taking action and calling out the poor behaviour to address the situation.

To me, this was not something that I could tolerate. It was worth following up and taking action to call out poor behaviour, especially from those in a senior leadership position. I was less concerned with the impact on me, but more about how the same situation could have played out with other people in the teams.

In a one-to-one with my boss, I expressed my concerns about someone at board level behaving like that in a meeting, the message it sends to the teams, the culture it breeds, and so on. My boss advised me to speak to the individual directly, expressing to them how they had made me feel in the meeting and to hold them to account. I was amused at this suggested course of action because this completely missed the point I was making. While I was irritated at how I had been spoken to and belittled, my concern was not about me as an individual. My point was about the culture, the environment and what behaviour was considered as acceptable in the organisation.

I left the one-to-one disappointed and frustrated that my concerns were not really heard, and the option to speak to the individual directly would not address what I feared was a bigger issue. I knew I wanted to push this subject further.

So, I decided to send a message on Microsoft Teams to my boss and the MD explaining what happened, what my concerns were and laying out what I felt was a cultural issue that needed to be addressed from an executive leadership perspective. My message was clear: "This isn't about me; it's about a concern of a growing toxic culture with behaviours being displayed by members of your leadership team that neither align with the company values nor with the culture the organisation is working to create."

I will be completely honest with you here. Sending a message to the boss and the person leading the whole company, calling out bad behaviour from someone on the board, caused me a lot of anxiety. I asked myself questions such as:

- "Is this a career-limiting message?"
- "Will they think I'm being a dick?"
- "Is this going to cause me problems in the workplace?"

But I knew that for me to be true to who I am, my values and be myself, it was something that I needed to address.

The response I received was disappointing. And the point was missed again.

The MD advised me to speak to the individual directly to address their behaviour towards me.

This left me in a situation where I needed to decide what to do next, and the same three questions were flying around in my head as I responded to the message. Potentially, the response I needed to give was going to create more of a conflict situation, or a career-limiting one. This is because I needed to highlight the missing of the point by both my line manager and the MD. This caused me to feel more anxious than it would have been to address the person who had been rude in the meeting.

I strapped on my bravest pants, threw caution to the wind, and replied with something along the lines of:

> *Thank you both for your response.*

> *While I appreciate your advice and I respect what you're suggesting, it is not a course of action that I am going to take.*
>
> *I believe that following your advice will actually damage my relationship with the person in question, which is not conducive to a positive working environment, and as such, not something I'm prepared to pursue.*
>
> *I raised the issue with you not because I am upset about how someone has treated me as an individual, but because the behaviours the individual has displayed are contradictory to the values of the organisation. And my concern is that this behaviour is not an isolated incident – there may be other individuals in the organisation who have experienced the same or worse. The concern is that this is not the culture or environment that should be fostered or behaviour accepted within the senior leadership team.*

I cannot tell you how many times I read and re-read the message to make sure it was as professional as possible while being clear and to the point. My palms after pressing send were beyond sweaty! I did not receive a response to my message, but I did not really expect to. Calling out bad behaviour was more important to me than getting a reply because I knew that in order to hold my head up and be truly who I was, standing up for what I knew and believed to be right was paramount.

You see, the confronting situation with the perpetrator was open conflict, whereas having to raise my head about the parapet with my boss and the MD felt like I was walking into a situation that was disguised conflict. I was not just calling out poor behaviour from the person who made the unacceptable comment, I was also calling out poor leadership in the approach suggested to me to resolve the issue. My point was this: "I'm a big girl; I can handle the situation with the person in question, but there is a bigger issue at hand, and you, as the leaders of the organisation, should be addressing those in your reporting line who are creating a psychologically unsafe and toxic environment." Simply put, it was not my issue to fix, and cultural issues within the senior leadership team needed to be dealt with by the senior leadership team. The inability to do so amounted to poor leadership, and showed a lack of experience, maturity or ability to deal with conflict by those people whose position made it THEIR responsibility to do so.

Something that I learned from the situation was that next time I was an active member of a meeting but also offering to play a supporting role to keep the minutes, I would set the rules of engagement and fair play at the outset of the meeting. Ensuring that my role, and those of the other attendees, were clear, as though setting out a meeting charter or expectations of the etiquette required from everyone present.

It was at around this point in my career that I had an epiphany about validation from others. About how during my early career as a woman in tech, I had compromised more of myself than I needed to, or wanted to. About trying to fit in, trying not to stand out, trying to be 'one of the lads' and squash down parts of who I was, which was no longer something I was prepared to do.

How do you break down the barrier where there is pressure to conform?

- Find ways to get your message across, even if it differs from that of others.

- Question the status quo and ask, "Why do we do it like that?"
- Stand firm with your boundaries and hold true to your values.
- Understand what battles are worth fighting for.
- Escalate where needed, seeking support and guidance from peers and leaders.

To quote Dr Seuss:

> *"Why fit in when you were born to stand out?"*

It is OK to stand out from the crowd – just because others conform, it does not mean you have to, too. One of my good friends and a respected colleague, has a picture of this quote on the wall of her office – something that is clearly visible when she is on video conference calls. It is an excellent statement message and sets the standards and expectations of those people on calls with her.

> **Tip:**
>
> **Standing out from the crowd can be scary, daunting and nerve-wracking. It is also empowering, freeing and exciting!**

**Fear of judgement or backlash**

There is no quick way to fight the fear of being judged or the concern that there will be negative repercussions resulting from your actions and shared opinions, possibly leading to your regretting of them. Battling this barrier is something that will take time and constant reinforcing of the boundaries you create to maintain a healthy approach.

## 8: Breaking down the barriers – Defying the norm

The story you have just read about the pressure to conform is equally as relevant to this barrier, as there was definitely a fear of backlash from standing up for myself and saying "no, I don't want to take your advice because I don't think it's the right thing for me to do". There were no obvious repercussions from the situation, but I wonder if it did make an impression on one of the two people that impacted my career a few years later.

To discuss breaking down this barrier, we are going to go back in time to when I was a little girl to share a story that I am not entirely proud of but will give you an example of how the fear of judgement can get the better of you.

I grew up in a town called Aylesbury in Buckinghamshire. It is not in the 'posh' part of the county, like Marlow and all the surrounding villages, where there is more wealth and people speak 'properly'. Aylesbury is a commuter town, located an easy travelling distance from London and Birmingham. It is a town that is close to the Chiltern Hills and surrounded by farmland. For those of us who were born and bred in Aylesbury, our accent is one that sounds like a strange mix of south London (read Sowf London), Essex and the West Country. It was an accent that I was conscious of, with certain words pronounced in a way that I have been teased for over the years – here are some examples:

- Grass = grarss
- Milk = miwk
- School = skou

Growing up, my stepdad's parents lived in a beautiful village outside of Aylesbury called Little Horwood. Grandma and Grandpa were not from Buckinghamshire, and moved there later in life, but they came from a time and place where people spoke beautiful English – the Queen's English back then. I was always very conscious when we went to visit them that I wanted to speak 'properly', not that they cared in the slightest, but I wanted to show that I could talk nicely and not with an affected accent. I was always careful to not mimic how they sounded, but each visit, I would switch on an accent that felt like I was speaking 'properly'. As soon as I got home after the visit, I went straight back to speaking how I normally would.

In the UK, there is a fair amount of stigma and jovial mockery around certain accents, which comes with a level of judgement and often, mimicking how people sound. Some accents are proclaimed 'beautiful' and for others, there is an association with a lack of intelligence. I am sure this same level of judgement and prejudice exists in countries all around the world, too. Knowing this perception of how people speak and sound, and what that means about their level of intellect, really struck me hard when I was younger. I was always conscious that while intelligent, my intelligence differed from other members of my family. I was never someone that others would consider 'book smart', although I love to learn, and I would not be considered an academic individual.

I already considered myself an outsider, and the 'black sheep' of the family, and I did not want the way I spoke or my accent to further compound being on the periphery. Interestingly, my brother never seemed concerned about his accent or anything along those lines – of the two of us, I always viewed him as popular, confident and outgoing. I wanted to fit in and, when it came to going to university, I made the conscious decision to change my accent permanently. What had been the 'switched on' accent was going to become how I sounded all the time.

To add some additional context to this decision, let me explain a little more about why I did this.

When I finished my GCSEs at 16 (I did not do particularly well – it turns out that revising is a good idea and something I had not bothered to do), I opted to study socio and economic history and English literature A levels at sixth form. I should add here that I did not study history at GCSE level and was not really sure of what to do at A level. I could not do any of the sciences because I had opted to do foundation science at GCSE to allow me to study what were then my passions of music and drama (not my best decision, but hey ho).

I chose English literature because I love to read but it transpired that poetry and I are not friends. After six months of studying A levels, I realised that the mode of study did not suit me, and I decided to 'drop out' of sixth form. I enrolled at the local college to study business studies instead. It was a different type of course than A levels, which followed a modular approach and was much more aligned with my learning style. Making this decision meant I had inadvertently taken a gap year and if I chose to go to university, it would be a year after the people who had finished their GCSEs at the same time as me.

At the end of my time at college, everyone was talking about university. I did not have a burning desire to study for three or four more years, but I also did not know what else to do. I am not lucky enough to have a vocation. On a whim, I applied to Oxford Brookes University to study business and management for four years. I figured that I may as well spend more time in the academic world, meet new people and maybe then I would figure out what to be when I grew up.

## 8: Breaking down the barriers – Defying the norm

Oxford is world-renowned for its hallowed university, although Oxford Brookes was not in the mix there as the old polytechnic. It was still a good university, but not one of the Russell Group universities in the UK. Oxford is in the next county over from Aylesbury and people spoke 'properly' there. I was worried that I would start of my university career on the wrong footing if I spoke like I came from Aylesbury. I was going to be meeting people from around the country, and I wanted to give myself the best chance of being accepted. So, from day one at university, I switched on the 'proper' accent.

I did not feel that it was inauthentic to make this change; it felt at the time like I was embracing my concerns about myself to make a positive change. Upon reflection, many years later, I question the decision I made and wonder what would have happened if I had not changed my accent. Would it really have impacted me the way I feared it would?

Today, my accent is not the one I had growing up. It is also not the 'proper' one I switched on. Having lived in Yorkshire for over 20 years, it is not a Yorkshire accent, either. I get teased for sounding 'posh' when I come from a working-class background and certainly did not grow up in a wealthy or affluent household. When I speak to my family, who still live in the south, they say I sound 'northern'. My accent is pretty non-descript so you would not be able to tell where I originally come from in England.

Now let us ask the obvious question: "Sophie, did changing your accent result in you fitting in more and being accepted?"

The answer would be a big, fat: "No."

I was so hung up on fitting in, being accepted based on how I sounded and what that would imply about my intelligence, that I did not realise that the facets about me that encouraged accepting and like-minded responses were down to my personality, my outlook on life, my values and my intelligence (albeit not classically 'academic').

Let us ask another question: "Sophie, how do you feel about your behaviour being led by a fear of judgement?"

The answer to this is relatively simple. I believe that all humans have a desire to 'fit in', to belong and to be accepted. It is commonplace in our younger years to behave in ways that we believe are more likely to result in positive affirmation from our peer group and those whose opinions we care about. Changing my accent was a learning journey and a point in time that I can reflect on and consider. Hindsight is a wonderful thing.

Let us ask one final question: "Sophie, do you regret changing your accent?"

I will be blunt: no I do not. But that is not because I think it was a good decision. I do not regret my decision because ultimately, I do not think there is any point in regretting it. I do not have a time machine. I cannot change the past. I made a decision with the best intentions and with the facts that I believed to be true at the time. If I came to a crossroads in my life today with the same decision before me, would I choose the same thing as I did as an 18-year-old? No, but that is because I have 30 years of experience under my belt and I know that how someone speaks, how they sound, the language they use, etc. does not define how intelligent they are and if someone chooses to judge based on a such a basic and irrelevant factor, then perhaps they need to consider the level of judgement they apply when dealing with others.

**Tip:**

> **There is no point regretting the past. It is done and you cannot change it. What you can do is use that knowledge to allow you to make better decisions in the future.**

What the example we have walked through here does not do is talk about the fear of backlash specifically. In life, there are always consequences to your actions, be they positive or negative. Sometimes, you will take a course of action with the best intentions, and it will fall flat. Other times, you will take a course of action knowing it may not be the best decision and may not have the result you want, but you do it anyway. The point is that there is no way of knowing the outcome until you try (unless you are doing something illegal where the consequences are pretty obvious, and you should not do it).

To take a hammer to this barrier and break it down, you need to consider the following and act accordingly:

- Who is judging you?
- Are they in a position of authority and can judge you?
- How much do you care about their judgement of you?
- Have you done your research?
- Do you know what the outcome will be?
- What is the worst that can happen?
- What are you afraid of? (Go back and read chapter 5!)

If you consider these questions and what they mean when it comes to being who you truly are – being your authentic self, it is time to strap on those brave pants. You only get one shot at this thing called life, so why choose to let fear drive how you live it?

## Under-representation and perceptions of leadership

More and more, we are seeing representation of people who look like us in positions of power, authority or in the mainstream media. The best example of this would be in film and television, where there are more people from a wider range of cultures, societies, genders, etc. Basically, I am saying it is not just white men at the top. This is becoming truer in the workplace, although I still do not see enough representation of women in leadership roles in the technology industry.

Rather than using a specific story or scenario to discuss this barrier, I am going to walk through my career to talk about the leadership and representation of women in the companies I worked for, with a specific focus on the technology industry. The following figures are a series of graphs for various organisations I have worked at, which show the representation of the following in percentages:

- Women in the technology team;
- Men in the technology team;
- Women in technology leadership roles; and
- Men in technology leadership roles.

These organisations are in no particular order in terms of when I worked within them during my career, and they are organisations of:

- Varying size (350 employees, c40,000 employees); and
- Different industry sectors (financial services, retail, betting and gaming, etc.)

## Organisation #1

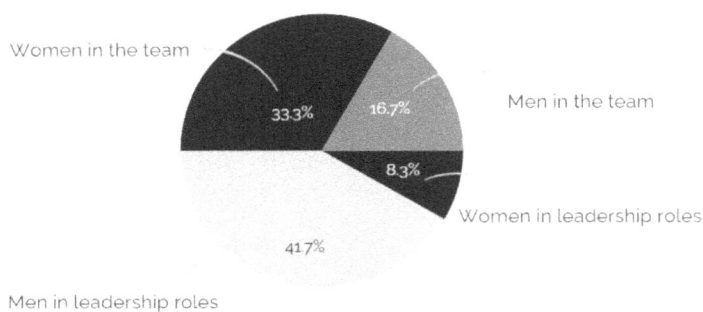

Women in the team

33.3%

16.7%

Men in the team

8.3%

Women in leadership roles

41.7%

Men in leadership roles

**Figure 9: Organisation #1**

## Organisation #2

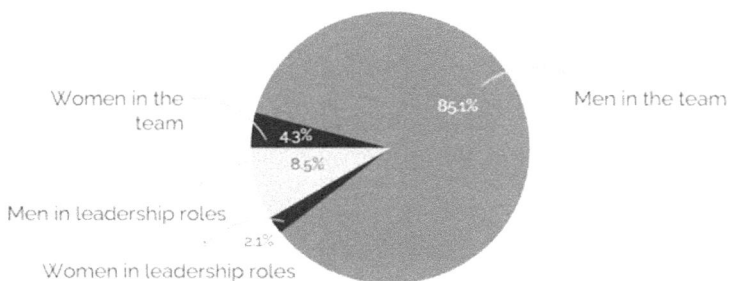

Women in the team

85.1%

Men in the team

4.3%

8.5%

Men in leadership roles

2.1%

Women in leadership roles

**Figure 10: Organisation #2**

## Organisation #3

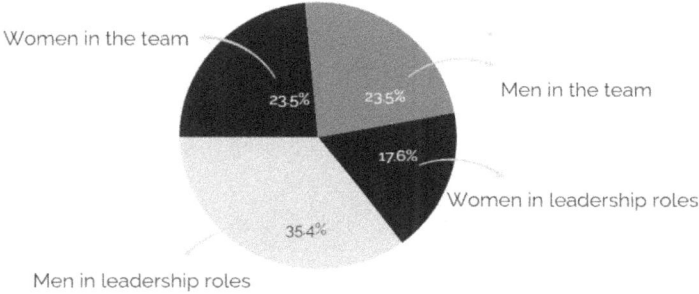

**Figure 11: Organisation #3**

## Organisation #4

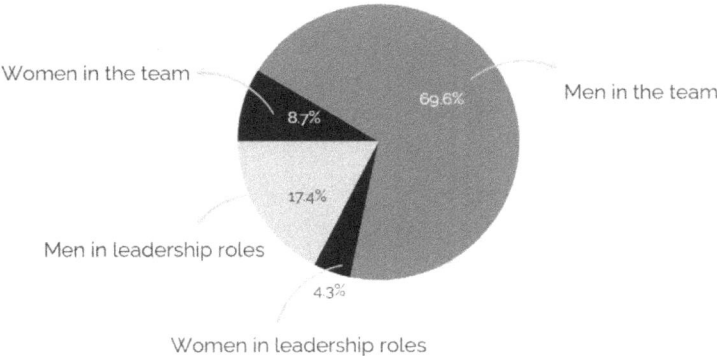

**Figure 12: Organisation #4**

Organisation #5

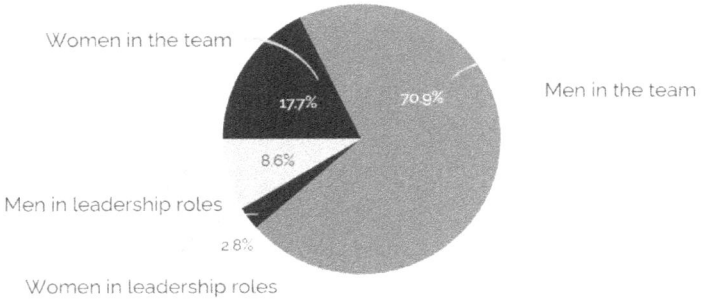

Women in the team

17.7%

70.9%

Men in the team

8.6%

Men in leadership roles

2.8%

Women in leadership roles

**Figure 13: Organisation #5**

Organisation #6

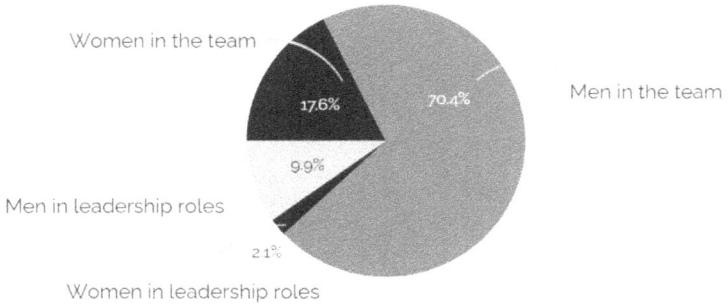

Women in the team

17.6%

70.4%

Men in the team

9.9%

Men in leadership roles

2.1%

Women in leadership roles

**Figure 14: Organisation #6**

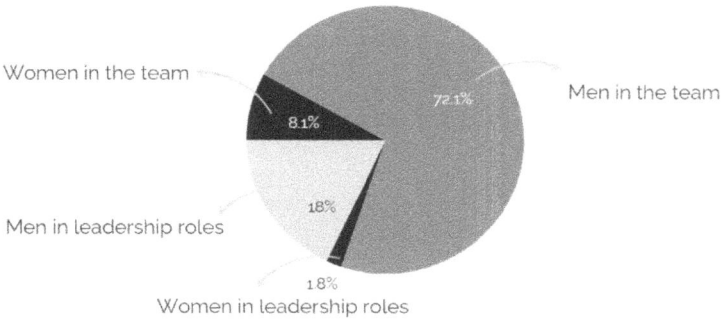

**Figure 15: Organisation #7**

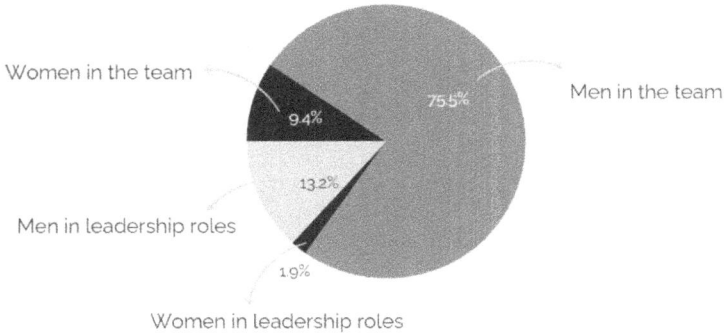

**Figure 16: Organisation #8**

Organisation #9

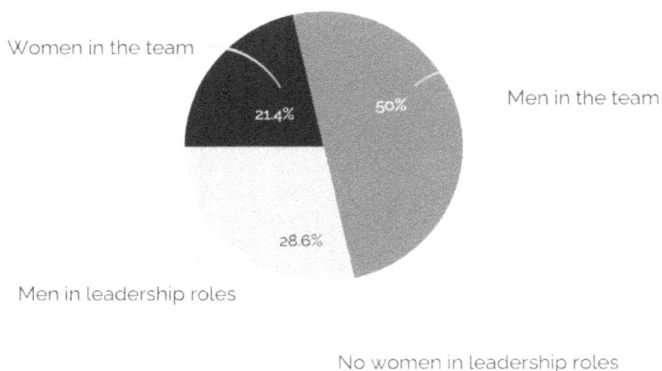

Women in the team

21.4%

50%

Men in the team

28.6%

Men in leadership roles

No women in leadership roles

**Figure 17: Organisation #9**

Unsurprisingly, the majority of the technology workforce is male. This is something that we know to be true. There is also the expected disparity between men and women in the leadership roles.

So, what is the problem here?

Why are there more men in technology than women? Why are there more men in technology leadership roles than women? Is there something wrong?

We need to go back in time a little to answer these questions:

- In the 1940s–60s, computing and programming was typically classed as secretarial or clerical work, which was an area predominantly filled by women – an excellent example are the women who worked for

NASA during the space race working as 'computers'. However, as the importance of computing grew, more men entered the industry.

- Turing et al were made famous for breaking the Enigma code during the Second World War in Bletchley Park. But at its peak in 1945, Bletchley Park was the home to around 10,000 people – 75% of whom were women working in various roles, including direct cryptanalysis.

- In the 1970s and 1980s, personal computers were marketed as toys for boys, furthering the societal norm that to be interested in computers was something reserved for men. Boys would be given computers as toys, whereas girls were still given dolls, kitchen sets, etc., aligned with the pink and blue approach to male and female interests.

- Gender stereotypes and bias exist in television, film and other media. Hackers, programmers and engineers were often roles filled by male actors, again furthering the idea that working in technology was for men.

- In both higher education and the workplace, there have historically been more men in specific industries and fields. For some, trying to be break into that field can be incredibly daunting.

**Workplace inequality**

I have often been heard saying that I have the biggest balls of anyone in the technology department and maybe the company. These are metaphorical testicles, but the meaning is the same (although as a feminist, I do reject the idea that to have courage and gumption, you need to be both male and have testicles). Why do I say this? I am not trying to play some form of one-upmanship. I am trying to challenge the narrative in the office to highlight that women are strong, powerful and capable, and that people should not be judged or characterised by their anatomy.

We already know that I have worked in the technology industry for my entire adult career across a range of sectors (including software development, manufacturing, financial services, retail, betting and gaming, etc.). We also know that this is predominantly a male industry. We know that the gender pay gap exists across all industries and sectors. We know that there is a difference between how women and men approach applying for jobs, with women often holding back if they do not hold the majority (if not all) of the qualifications whereas typically men will still apply for a role if they do not have all the required qualifications or skills.

An article published by Harvard Business School in 2024, called "Breaking Through the Self-Doubt That Keeps Talented Women from Leading",[31] talks about why women are less likely to apply for jobs and what approaches employers can use to empower women and bring in more talent to their organisation. One area that I have helped clients with is rewriting job descriptions to include more inclusive language and terminology that would appeal to a wider pool of candidates. It is surprising how many job descriptions include male-oriented language and make reference to "him" or "he" when talking about the ideal candidate. Organisations can become inadvertently oblivious

---

[31] *https://www.library.hbs.edu/working-knowledge/breaking-through-the-self-doubt-that-keeps-talented-women-from-leading?.*

to the language used and how that may deter potential talented candidates.

So, how do you break down this barrier when it comes to being authentic?

As always, I am going to be completely honest with you – this one is tricky. I cannot say in all certainty that I have been able to break through the inequalities that exist. But I will tell you that I have given it a bloody good go and will continue to try. Here is an example of where I have chipped away at the imbalance while maintaining both my professionalism and being true to what I believe in.

I had been promoted to the senior leadership team in the technology department in a team that was mostly male. I was particularly proud of the promotion as it had come about because I had presented a proposal to change the strategic approach to service management to my boss and the CIO. I proposed that we should align with the other regions, which each had a dedicated service management function, and that by doing the same in the UK, we would ensure the appropriate service mindset throughout the UK business, rather than being diluted under an existing pillar.

In my previous role, I had not realised how much lower than the market rate I was being paid until it was too late. During a previous promotion, my line manager at the time sadly was not as much of an advocate for equal pay as I would have liked, so moving into the head of service management role, I was being paid a lower salary than average, both in terms of average within the organisation and my peer group, and in the wider industry as a whole. As is often the case, internal promotions come with a restriction on how much of a salary increase you can get, despite the industry benchmark for the role. Speaking with my new boss, we agreed an approach that would upscale my salary to something closer to the benchmark, but it would be done in increments over time.

Something I should share here is that at this point in the role, the actual benchmark had not been shared with me. The organisation, like so many others, kept this a mysterious secret and chose not to share salary benchmarking with their employees. However, I did a check on LinkedIn to see what the benchmark was in both Yorkshire and the UK and I knew that my salary was significantly lower. I still felt incredibly lucky, though, to be earning a good salary and have the recognition of being able to build the service management function from scratch.

Fast forward two years and I still held the same position in the senior leadership team, with the same title. The previously agreed increases in my salary had taken place within the first 6 months in the role and each year I had received the typical 3% increase given to all employees. I was deputising for the CIO on a regular basis as well as working closely with him to help:

- Build the strategy of the function;
- Build the board reports, setting the tone and message for the board meetings;
- Take the lead with the leadership team to drive engagement and a collaborative cross-function approach; and
- Reignite the colleague-engagement approach with revitalised town halls, annual awards and working groups to all colleagues to input into the direction of the function.

This was not everything, but it gives you a flavour of how my career and responsibilities had progressed along with my standing in the senior leadership team. However, something that always irked me, but I never said anything about, was while I was deputising for the CIO, attending meetings on his behalf and delivering CIO-level reporting and strategies, I was not the named contact in his out-of-office message. That honour was given to one of my male peers. It is something I wish now that I had asked about, but at the time, I let it slide, thinking that I did not need the additional 'glory' of the named escalation point in the event of the CIO being absent.

The person who was named in these out-of-office messages and I got on famously. We worked well together as a team – we had different styles and approaches to leadership, but we found a happy balance. As part of the relationship with him, it came out in a conversation that he was paid significantly more than me and yet I had more responsibility. When I say 'significantly more', I am not talking about a few thousand pounds' difference, I am talking tens of thousands more than I was being paid.

This pissed me off.

I needed to figure out how to address the ridiculous disparity between how me and my male peers were being paid.

Talking about salaries and asking for a pay rise is no small thing. I had a great relationship with the CIO, but I also knew it was not going to be an easy conversation for me to have. Like I said a moment ago, I was glad to be earning a good salary and the opportunity that came with it, giving me experience that would be a great foundation to further my career. I was levelling up experience-wise, and I had my sights on potentially breaking into the C-suite for my next role, but needed to make a strong argument for increased remuneration with my boss.

I decided to ask the question in my regular one-to-one and test the water to see what would happen. My boss was really great about the conversation, but the answer was "no". There was no increase available, no budget, no option to reduce the pay gap. I accepted his response as I knew how things worked in the organisation but also made it clear that I would keep asking. It was outside of his control and I could appreciate this.

Periodically, I would raise the question in my one-to-ones, but the answer was always the same.

A few months later, the team expanded and another 'Head of' joined our fold. I discovered that this person was walking into a salary that was again tens of thousands of pounds more than my salary. The role they were filling was one that is typically paid more than a head of service management, but not by THAT much. There was another woman on the senior leadership team, too, who had not been given the 'Head of' title but had similar responsibilities as the rest of the team. While I never knew the exact amount, I knew she was being paid less than everyone else.

This boiled my blood. The two women on the team were being paid less than the men. OK, there were other factors like the role title and how the wider technology industry recognises certain roles, but to have such a vast gap was just not right, nor acceptable.

I increased the frequency of my requests for a salary increase. By this, I mean that I literally asked in every one-to-one with my boss, which was every two weeks. I was done playing nice and compliant. I wanted to be treated fairly and paid in accordance with my peers. As always, my boss explained the situation and his hands were tied. My asking became a bit of a running joke, but I did not back down. I despise any form of inequality and as I have said previously, I will fight battles that are worth fighting. What happened next only heightened my dogged behaviour.

I was shown the benchmark for my role.

Not only was I not within the entire benchmark, but I was also not even close to the bottom 'entry level' range of the benchmark. The top of the range was still lower than what my male peers were being paid, but it was less than £10,000 of difference. Can you imagine the astonishment, the rage, the shock, my incredulity at this?

In each of my annual performance reviews since joining the company, I had achieved 'exceeds expectations' – the top level of performance, delivering all my role requirements and more. In order to be entry level in a role, you typically would receive a lower rating in your annual performance review with objectives to focus your personal development to be able to be performing as expected. I knew this because I was a people manager and had to manage the expectations of my own team members. I needed to speak to my boss about the benchmark and ask with more sincerity about an increase that reflected both my performance and my standing in the organisation.

So, I asked and was told that I was 'entry level' and that there would be no increase. There was no room for me to comment here or plead my case.

What did I do next?

Well, I continued to ask for a salary increase in my one-to-ones. The running joke continued, although it was no longer as funny. Also, when I was asked to do things that would be considered above 'entry level', I would openly comment that I could not possibly get involved as I was entry level and did not have the experience or seniority to be able to handle the additional responsibility. I was not trying to be difficult, and I would always do what was asked of me, but I felt that I needed to make a point. To make it abundantly clear that I should not be asked to do these advanced tasks if I was considered entry level. Did that change anything? No.

Fast forward again to the end of 2021, and there was an organisational change on the horizon that would mean that my role as head of service management would no longer exist, and I was put at risk of redundancy. The structure changes meant there would be a group-level service management role that I could step into so that I would not be made redundant. This role carried a narrower remit than my UK-focused role but carried the weight of 'Group', which transversed three regions, so from the outside looking in, was considered a more senior role and in theory had more responsibility.

But guess what…

The salary was only £10,000 more a year than my current salary, which only just took me into the 'entry level' banding for the benchmarking of my old role. This new salary was for me only – anyone external to the organisation would have been offered market rate. Yes, you read that right – the salary increase was still nowhere near the salaries of my UK-based peers and was nowhere near the salary available for similar roles in the marketplace in the UK and across Europe.

I declined the offer of both the role and the salary increase. Whilst the salary was one of the deciding factors for declining it, there was other factors that helped make the decision. My role was made redundant and I took the opportunity to start my own consultancy.

What is the lesson here? How does this link into being authentic? Referring back to my values, there are three that stand out specifically, which are:

- Integrity
- Courage
- Family

In terms of integrity here, it was about standing up for something I believed to be right and important. Women should not be paid less than men for the same or similar roles. The facts were that the two women in the leadership team were paid the least amount of money. Something I had not included in the above is that there was a member of my team who earned about £2,000 less than I did without any of the responsibility and accountability I had. And yes, the team member was a man. I am not saying that the organisation I worked for was inherently sexist, in fact their diversity, equity and inclusion (DEI) programme was pretty good. However, there were gaps in the organisation in terms of female leadership and they did not always seem to care to fill these gaps either because of restrictive and unrealistic processes or due to a lack of awareness.

It is essential to pause to consider the fact here that standing up for something does not mean you will get the outcome you would like. It doesn't not automatically mean that you will "win". I wasn't disappointed at the outcome; I understand that some things were well beyond my control and influence. Personally, the "win" was to have the voice, the courage and conviction to stand up for what I felt was important.

It took courage to have the first conversation about potentially increasing my salary. And through asking the question repeatedly, I removed some of the fear and stigma attached to asking such a forthright question. Do not get me wrong, there may be times ahead where I feel a sense of trepidation about having a conversation about money, but it will not be like it used to. Certainly, this experience has supported me as an independent consultant discussing day rates, pricing for fixed-term pieces of work, etc. in ways that it may have taken me a little longer had this situation not occurred.

Lastly, family. This does not mean in the typical usage of the word. Family, to me, means something more, as we discussed in chapter 4. For me, in relation to this whole situation, it was about the sisterhood. About standing up for the women in the organisation who were not represented at the leadership level or did not have a platform for their voices to be heard. There were female leaders through the organisation, but as for the technology function, there were only the two of us. We were support for one another – I was typically more vocal about the inequalities and refused to accept them and ended up leaving the organisation. This is possibly from being brought up by such a strong, independent woman like my mum who was an advocate for women and women's rights both professionally and personally.

For you, what would breaking down the barriers of workplace inequality to allow you to be authentic look like? It could be:

- Understanding your boundaries and where the line must be drawn when it comes to inequalities in the workplace;

- Understanding when, where, how and to whom you are prepared to raise your head above the parapet and say "this is not OK" or "we must do better" or "why don't we…";
- Understanding your values and where you want to hold true to them, voicing your opinion; and
- Understanding when it is time to either accept the situation or walk away.

None of these are easy things to do, especially if you work in an organisation that is filled to the rafters with one form of privilege or another. However, you are here on your journey to be more authentic at work, to bring out who you are, your passions and not to be afraid of showing that, so maybe you can start with bite-sized chunks.

**Imposter syndrome**

Imposter syndrome is a like a mosquito waiting for its moment to strike, or just a psychological bully.

How many times have you had the thoughts "I'm not good enough to do this" or "if maybe I was a little more like <insert person's name>, perhaps I'd be able to do that"? It is a horrid feeling, or state of being, to battle and there is no easy way to break that fucker down. It will take time, patience, and importantly, the ability to be kind to yourself and realise that actually you are good enough. That you do not need to be more like anyone else. And that you just need to be yourself and build the confidence to hold your head high to know that you have got this.

Let me give you an example of where imposter syndrome is constantly knocking at my door and trying to stop me from being truly authentic.

Working for myself requires me to be a 'jack of all trades' in many respects: I am the lead consultant, the finance director, the sales and marketing director, the web designer, the tech support, etc. When it comes to branding and putting myself out there, I see what those in my peer group do and I know that I need to do something similar, so long as it is in keeping with who I am and what I want to achieve.

> **Tip:**
>
> *"Jack of all trades, master of none, but oftentimes better than master of one."*
>
> **William Shakespeare**

People in my peer group do the following:

- Speak at conferences across the world;
- Deliver keynote speeches;
- Work with a plethora of clients;
- Create podcasts;
- Create content;
- Write articles;
- Act as recognised thought leaders for everything imaginable;
- Speak on podcasts;
- Host podcasts;
- Create and manage communities;
- Create frameworks and deliver training; and

- Post on social media with thousands of followers, subscribable content, newsletters, etc.

This list could go on.

And then there is me. I post on LinkedIn daily. I do speak at events, but it is not easy getting my submissions accepted; I am often a joint speaker with someone else or filling the spot that someone else (the first choice) is not available for. Yes, I have spoken on podcasts, and I have dabbled with writing articles, but it feels like a minuscule achievement compared to the activity of my peers. Quite frankly, I often feel small, insignificant, like I cannot compete with my peers and as though I am never going to break through to be a headliner or keynote speaker.

Let me be clear here, I have no desire to be one of the elite or have my name in lights, but I do want to continue building my brand and my reach. But this is where my imposter syndrome has kicked in and tells me that I am not good enough to compete.

Even writing this book, I have asked myself a million times: "Who am I to be writing a book?" And thought: "What if no one reads it?" When these questions arise, I have to force myself to shake off the imposter syndrome, to quieten the voice inside my head that tells me that I am not good enough and force my way through into the light of realisation that I AM. I do not need to do the same things as my peers. I do not need to be like anyone but Sophie. My version of success may look different to others and that is more than OK. So what if I am the second choice for speaking at a conference? I will be the best damned second choice they have ever had, so that next time around, perhaps I will be one of the first choices. So what if I do not have my own podcast yet (although this is something a friend and I have already discussed)? It is something that will come when time allows and we have the right topic.

The point here is that the barrier that is imposter syndrome is inside YOU. Any of the external influences that appear like they are holding you back for this barrier actually are not. It is your own belief in yourself and that self-assurance that you need to build to quieten that voice. It may be a work in progress to ignore that voice completely, and it may not be something that you ever truly conquer, but have faith in yourself. Back yourself and do not let fear or the weight of your self-criticism choose the path you are taking for yourself.

## Limited support networks

It has only been in more recent years that support networks have started appearing in organisations, be they dedicated for women in business, women in tech, diversity and inclusion, disabilities, LGBTQ+, etc. So it may be that you are working in an organisation and there is no support available to you. The same applies to internal mentoring programmes – they do not always exist, sometimes you have to apply to be a part of them, they are not always open to everyone in the organisation, and so on.

So, what do you do?

What is stopping you from creating your own support network with other like-minded individuals?

This is not as hard as it may seem. You could speak to colleagues about starting a community of practice, or community of support. You could branch out and look to start something in the wider world, seeking support and offering membership to fellow professionals. LinkedIn is a great place to start, as is Substack.

Are there networks available in the wider world, outside of your organisation, that would be a good fit for you?

Maybe start with searching LinkedIn to see what groups are out there. Many of the support groups, organisations and communities also have a website. I know there are many like TechHer, SheCodes, itSMF's Women in ITSM, etc. (See the appendix for more details of these and other organisations mentioned in this chapter.)

A casual Internet search is going to bring up a gazillion options, too – there is a wealth of support out there that you could get involved in.

Are there professional bodies you can join where there are support groups?

Yes! There are many:

- *it*SMF UK
- BCS (British Computer Society)
- Association for Women in Computing
- SDI (Service Desk Institute)
- Open Service Community
- Scopism SIAM community
- And so many more!

The options are endless, and not all these professional bodies need you to pay large fees to join; some are free! You can also attend conferences (virtually or in person), where there are always stands hosted by support organisations and communities.

Are there mentoring programmes you can sign up for?

Of course! One I have been part of for many years is Reed's Women in Technology community (details in the appendix), which has a dedicated platform for mentees and mentors, and it puts the control in the hands of the mentee, which is fantastic. It is FREE to sign up and use. As any good mentoring programme should be, in my humble opinion.

Is there someone you know that would make a cracking mentor?

There is bound to be someone you know either in your organisation or wider network that you could ask. In total, I have seven mentees and only two of them are through a mentoring programme. The others are people whom I have either worked with before who have asked me to be their mentor or they know of me through their network of connections in LinkedIn and they have approached me.

There is nothing wrong with asking someone to be your mentor. The worst thing they can say is "no" and if they do say no, it is most likely because of availability or something else that is wholly unconnected to you asking them. And they could say "yes!". What are you waiting for?

> **Hint:**
> **There is more specific advice and guidance on mentoring and things you should know in chapter 9.**

## Sexual harassment and discrimination

Sadly, there are a whole host of examples here that I could write about, including comments on how I am dressed, being smacked on the backside, suggestive remarks, misogynistic statements, and so on.

**Sexual harassment**

I contributed one story to a book published in 2024 called *Allyship Actually*, written by Lucy Grimwade and David Barrow, which features 18 months of being stalked by a co-worker and how that played out. The book is a compelling read, where the stories shared are all real-world examples of harassment and discrimination in the workplace. The discussion on allyship, what it is, and how to be an ally, is incredibly powerful and thought-provoking. It is a great resource and, personally, I believe that all organisations should invest in obtaining copies, sharing with their teams to continue to drive positive change and equity in the workplace.

While I will not repeat the same story here as I would advise you to read that book, here are the key points:

- I was stalked for 18 months by a male co-worker.
- I was concerned about my reputation so I did not report it for a long time.
- I discovered that I had allies in unexpected places.
- Asking for help took courage, but it had positive results.
- The blocking feature on social media and mobile phones is useful.

I was talking about the situation recently because I have learned that my stalker has also potentially harassed other women in the workplace. I was asked if I reported the behaviour to the HR department, as sexual harassment constitutes gross misconduct in most (if not all) organisations, which would have meant there were repercussions for the perpetrator. I had to admit that I did not report it through the official channels but should have done.

Why did I not officially report it? Partly because I felt that I could manage the situation by myself, but also because I was concerned about victim-blaming. Having worked in such a male-dominated environment for a long time, I would joke and laugh with my colleagues, but it was never flirtatious (not from my perspective anyway). While my boundaries were firm, there were occasions in previous organisations where I had had to address rumours of sexual relationships with my male colleagues. These rumours were complete fiction. They originated from people who could not understand how a woman could work in a stereotypically male industry, and get promoted, based on talent and merit.

The experiences from my past haunted me. I felt my reputation had been tarnished and when the stalking began, I did not want those old rumours to be resurrected in the company I was working in. I did eventually tell my manager what was happening, and the situation was dealt with inside the confines of the technology department, without going through the formal channels. I should have fought through my fears. I should have escalated the sexual harassment through the appropriate process to ensure that the individual was held accountable for their actions.

### *Sexual discrimination*

The real-world example we will discuss for this part of the barrier is going to come from a source that I did not see coming.

As women, we travel through this world almost expecting a level of harassment and discrimination in the workplace and typically, we expect it to come from the men in the organisation. Most women have had to deal with unwanted advances in and outside of work. Most women have had comments and remarks shouted at them in the street in the form of 'cat calling'. What is less commonplace and rarely expected is when harassment and discrimination come from your fellow female colleagues.

This story has two parts, which happened on separate occasions but involved the same person behaving in a discriminatory way.

**Part one:**

Going back roughly 20 years, I was deputy team leader of a technical infrastructure and desktop support team. To add context of what this means in reality, 'desktop support' is the IT way of saying the people who look after your computer, your screen and any of the applications you use on it. When talking about 'infrastructure', I mean the connectivity that enables you to have email and access it and to have telephones (although, these days having a telephone on your desk is becoming rarer) and ensuring everything works in the background that enables you to do your job.

Part of my responsibilities was being a mentor to two apprentices. They had joined the organisation as part of a government-backed programme to support young people from under-privileged backgrounds to enter the workforce to gain skills and experience, setting them up for a career that would support changing their personal circumstances. This was something I took very seriously and was the start of dedicating my personal time to being a mentor to others, giving back where I can and supporting people in a way that was not available to me when I was young.

In addition to being a mentor, it was my responsibility to ensure that any new members of the team had learned the necessary skills and processes to resolve the issues people had with their computers as well as supporting the company network. I had written all the process documentation and built a knowledgebase that allowed anyone joining the team to get up to speed quickly, enabling them to do their jobs. All of this was in addition to managing incidents and requests myself.

On one particular day, June (not her real name) had logged an issue with her computer, and it was not something that we could fix over the phone. As it was a great learning opportunity for the two apprentices, we all went to the part of the office building where June worked, and I explained what the issue was and what I suspected to be the cause.

We arrived en masse at June's desk, ready to start investigating. Anyone who provides IT support services that is worth their weight will know that the best way to start an investigation is to speak to the end user or customer (the person who is having the issue) to understand:

- What happened;
- What they were doing at the time of the issue; and
- Further details (to get a clear picture of what occurred).

All this is done to enable swifter troubleshooting and remediation. I greeted June and advised what we were there for and started asking questions. Each time I asked a question, June directed her answers at the two male apprentices I had taken with me. She did not make eye contact with me, nor face me.

Before continuing, it is worth noting that June and I had had many interactions in the previous two years of me working there. She knew who I was, what I did and what my position in the IT department was.

## 8: Breaking down the barriers – Defying the norm

Back to the story. Anyone who has been in one of these situations will know how utterly frustrating it is to have someone ignore you as the person asking the questions, and direct the answers to a man, as though the woman is not there and the man must have seniority, greater experience and skill. In these situations, I usually ignore the behaviour and crack on with the job at hand. I find not pandering to the behaviour works reasonably well, and if it gets to the point where it is really annoying, I will make sure I use the person's name when asking the questions to try to direct their attention back to me as the person they are interacting with.

I did not feel the need to do that on this occasion because halfway through asking the questions, June turned her head towards me and said, "Can you fix this as well as the boys?", nodding in the direction of the two apprentices as she said it.

I should also add that June was not known for a sense of humour or making tongue-in-cheek remarks. So when she asked this question, I knew she was seriously questioning my ability over the two lads I was mentoring.

It was a bit of a shock that someone was being so openly discriminatory to me and all women working in technology. I was not prepared for the question. I was not amused by the tone nor the inference of the question, as well as it potentially undermining my position with the two apprentices. I knew that how I answered was going to be important.

There are so many ways I could have answered, some of which are less polite than others, but I went with this option: "Yes, actually, because I am teaching them all I know." It was a slight mic-drop moment as she had not expected me to be blunt and answer quickly. She became rather quiet and I carried on with working through the issue with her computer and explaining the troubleshooting process to the two apprentices.

Sadly, this was not my only encounter with June.

**Part two:**

Fast forward about a year. I had recently become a mother for the first time and had returned to full-time work when my daughter was three months old. Not a decision that was taken lightly but sometimes, needs must – it is a decision I was and remain comfortable with.

Shortly after returning to work, I was going through the list of issues that had been raised with my team and came across an incident raised by June. I had not forgotten our encounter the year before but had hoped that there would be no further instances of discriminatory behaviour, especially to a fellow woman.

Oh, how wrong I was!

Again, it was an issue that required a visit to June's desk and off I went. This time I went by myself – the apprentices had passed all their exams, had been offered permanent positions in the team and had their own workload.

I managed a couple of questions before June started asking about my baby and how she was doing. As any pregnant woman or new mother will know, you get into a routine of answering the same questions over and over, with people who know you assuming some sort of right to know everything that is happening with your child (I could write a whole book on this topic alone!). I went through the usual motions until June said:

"I think it is disgraceful when women come back to work full-time after having a baby and leave their children with strangers at a nursery. And you've only had three months off. What kind of mother does that?"

I am sure, dear reader, whether you are someone with children or not, that you can imagine my outrage at such a disgusting, discriminatory and derogatory comment about me as both an individual and a parent. I can assure you that I wanted to tell her to 'go fuck herself', however, being a consummate professional, I somehow managed to rein myself in. I felt that I needed to respond, so I said:

"Not everyone has the luxury of being able to afford to stay at home full-time with their baby. Some people have to return to work to keep a roof over their head."

Unfortunately, my response was not enough to deter June from her attack on me as a woman and my role as a mother, and she responded with a slight snarl, saying:

"Well, back when I was a new mum, I would let cheques bounce and run the risk of losing my house so that my children had a dedicated parent bringing them up where they belong, at home with their mother."

My original desired response to June bubbled up in my mouth, but again somehow, I managed to restrain myself from a response that would probably get me fired, despite the provocation. Instead, this time, I decided not to try to justify my choices, which had nothing to do with June, but to try to take the wind out of her sails by simply saying "OK". I continued working on her computer and once fixed, walked away from her desk.

I cannot express in polite words how this interaction angered me and how I still feel about being spoken to like that by a fellow woman and mother. What I can tell you is that when I went back to my desk, I did not display the same level of professionalism as I had managed to muster while at June's desk, when recanting the tale to my colleagues. They were all equally shocked, but no one said anything about needing to raise the issue with HR or June's manager. I did not really know what to do about it, if I am honest, but I knew that in that moment, the words from someone completely unconnected to me made me feel like a failure as a woman and as a mother, and I felt a level of shame that I will never forget.

I did not do anything about what June said, but I can tell you that I NEVER answered the phone when she telephoned for IT support and the team all knew that any issues she raised would need to be dealt with by someone other than me. I simply refused to help someone as bigoted as she was. Not exactly behaviour to be proud of, particularly when one of my values is to act with integrity and live on the lofty planes of the moral high ground. But it is how I chose to manage the situation at the time.

Breaking down this barricade of sexual harassment and discrimination is no small feat and, in many ways, until we live in a truly equal society, I do not believe we will ever remove this barrier from being our authentic selves. However, what you can do when faced with it is:

- Maintain your professionalism;
- Try to avoid rising to the bait;
- Act according to your values;
- Escalate and report any form of harassment and/or discrimination; and
- Try not to allow the bigoted, narrow-minded opinions and thoughts of others stop you from being who you are.

> **Tip:**
>
> **If you are the subject of harassment or discrimination at work, report it. There will be policies and processes in place to protect you and action will be taken. You are not alone.**

## Emotional labour

This is quite an interesting topic to discuss, and it is going to take some doing to rein in my thoughts on the overt sexism in the workplace when it comes to 'working mums' and the lack of a 'working dads' label. We have already discussed the pink and blue jobs and my thoughts here, so I will endeavour to stay off the soap box and stick to the topic at hand.

I am a woman. I have children. I do have a maternal side, but I am not someone who had a biological clock or who gets broody at the sight of a baby. When my friends have children, I am the last person to rush over and ask to hold the baby. In fact, I would rather not. Yes, as a mother, I do hold my own children but that does not automatically mean I want to hold someone else's. I love my children dearly and I also love myself too. Being a parent is a facet of who I am but not the entirety of me – not by a long stretch. Why am I sharing this for this section? Well, we have already spoken about the time where I was berated for returning to work when my children were young babies, so the fact I have not followed the expected norm will not be a shock.

Now, imagine you are me at work and someone has brought their newborn baby in to say hello to the team. Let us go one step further and imagine that this person with the baby is someone I get on really well with. Where do you think I will be standing with the people greeting the person? Yes, you are right – I am at the back of the pack doing everything I can to not have a turn at holding the baby. In all honesty, I would be happy just smiling and waving from a distance and cracking on with whatever I am doing, but I know that would be considered rude. Particularly when the office where this is happening is one where I am the only woman in the IT team. There are expectations and comments when my behaviour differs from the 'norm'.

And to clarify, other people's children are fine, but when I hold someone else's baby, they always start crying and because I have children of my own, there is an expectation that I will calm the baby down. But I do not want to try to calm the baby, and I do not know how. I know what worked with my girls, but this is nearly two decades ago and I am rusty, quite content in the knowledge that this is a skill that I am happy to let diminish.

This is not particularly an example of emotional labour but it does give you further insight into a time when I have been my authentic self and doing so means going against the grain. It speaks of the expectation of women in the workplace, perhaps an example that is better suited in the "The pressure to conform" section, but bear with me.

When it comes to emotional labour in the workplace, there are some tasks or activities that are predominantly seen as 'women's work' or things where a woman would be better because of their ability to show empathy, their warmth, etc. Realistically, this is bullshit, and we have already discussed the joys of societal norms and gender stereotyping. So, what do you do in a situation where someone is expecting you to be behave in a particular way or to deliver a piece of work, or take the lead on something just because of your gender or another characteristic? It is not always easy to say "no".

In pretty much every role I have held, I have been someone that gets confided in. This is generally something that I love and feel honoured that someone trusts me enough to share their secrets or bring me in the loop on something confidential. I take this trust seriously and I do like to be a safe space for others. However, I have been used as a free counselling service by some colleagues in the past, where the weight of what they were sharing with me became an emotional drain that was hard to carry. I have been told about people's sex lives, their medical history, their mental-health challenges, relationship and marital difficulties, and so much more. There have been times where a member of my team has taken advantage of my empathetic nature to keep them from getting in trouble for poor performance.

To break through this barrier of expectation for me to behave in a particular way that is seen as nurturing or maternal, I have had to implement boundaries.[32] For example:

- Not connecting with anyone from work on social media apart from LinkedIn;
- Not going out on team dinners or events, or only going for the meal; and
- Distancing myself from personal conversations or discussions that would most likely call on me as the woman to fill a particular role in the conversation.

Sometimes when I have done this, I have been called 'cold' or 'intimidating'. Other times, colleagues have respected my

---

[32] Although, the success rate of these boundaries has differed based on people not respecting them, or the severity of the situation calling for the boundaries to be overstepped.

boundaries, but not always. It is a hard balance between doing all this and being an effective leader who is empathetic, who is engaged with the team and creates a positive environment.

As a leader, I believe that leading with empathy is non-negotiable. We all typically spend more time with our colleagues than our families, so I believe it is important to know about your team while maintaining a professional distance – for example, I remember birthdays, significant others' names, children's and pets' names, and ensure I make time to connect with my team members. The relationship I engage in is professional but human, friendly but with boundaries. And this is because it is important to be part of the team but not fill a specific gender-biased role because of my anatomy.

Having things like a team charter, setting boundaries and agreeing ways of working will help with this, as will ensuring that all members of the team take their turn taking meeting minutes and arranging nights out.

When it comes to being asked to do tasks that are emotionally heavy and/or you are being asked because of your gender, or whatever other reason, and you do not want to do it, you can say "no". You can suggest alternative solutions, people or options. You can even call out that the task being asked of you does not fit in your job description, if that is applicable. There is nothing wrong with saying you are uncomfortable performing a task or taking on additional workload that is nothing to do with your job, or if you feel like it is an unfair or biased request.

## Balancing professionalism and femininity

During my life so far, I have seen significant change in the language associated with women in the workplace, however, in many respects there is less advancement that I would have hoped. For example, it is a well-known fact that female actors are typically paid significantly lower than their male counterparts, and this is all the truer for people of colour in the acting profession being paid lower than either white men or white women.

We also know that when you look at industries like hospitality, there are more male chefs than female, and some of those women we do see in the top-tier executive chef roles are often referred to as ball-busters, or the language associated with them is either male-oriented or not complimentary – this is something we discussed earlier in this chapter when talking about bias in the workplace.

Now, when it comes to being a woman in a male-dominated environment and you want to maintain your authenticity, it can be difficult to find the right balance between professionalism and embracing your femininity. I have never considered myself to be a girly girl. I have always veered more towards 'Tom boy' interests and habits, and parts of my personality definitely resonate with that moniker. But that does not mean I am not feminine and it is important to me to embrace my femininity. It is tough being a woman and I am not afraid to say it.

Let us talk about the singer and performer who is Pink. Pink is an incredible role model for young girls, and all young people. She is creative, strong, powerful, intelligent and openly talks about the need to be yourself and to avoid conforming to the ideals of someone else, or of society. If you see her perform, you will see a fantastic display of feminine power and strength combined with an individual who is obviously serious about her profession – the personification of professionalism and femininity, in my opinion.

Jameela Jamil (a British actress, presenter, writer and activist) is another example of someone who is innately feminine and professional. She talks openly about women's rights, about things that have happened to her and about driving positive change. In the roles she fills, she is versatile and captivating. She is sexy, strong, powerful and openly vulnerable all at once. She is another person in the public eye who is the embodiment of the balance between professionalism and femininity.

Angela Rayner, the UK deputy prime minister at the time of writing this book, is a third example of this balance between being feminine and professional. Slammed in the tabloid media for her choice of brightly coloured suits and the videos of her dancing in the street during a parade, she nevertheless rises above it to continue to be herself and also do her job, advocating for the UK population. Interestingly, the former prime minister of Finland, Sanna Marin, was also slammed in some tabloid media for dancing at a private party yet she was a positive addition to the Finnish government and role model for girls and women worldwide.

These are just some examples of women in the public eye who display a fantastic balance between being professional and embracing their femininity. As I do not know any of these women personally, I cannot ask the question of them about any difficulty they experience around being authentic, and the balance of these two things in a male-dominated world. However, I can talk about how to break this barrier down.

To be feminine does not mean being weak, negatively emotional or an inability to progress in your career.

To be professional does not mean being cold, dictatorial, to lack emotion or empathy.

I embrace my femininity through how I do my hair or eye make-up, and in the clothes I wear. For you, how you choose to embrace what is feminine is entirely up to you.

# CHAPTER 9: INVESTING IN THE BANK OF YOU

> **Practical steps to help you invest in yourself, build who you are, embrace your authenticity and be proud of it.**

There are parts of this chapter that are more about finding yourself, investing time in you and your needs than specifically focusing on your authenticity journey. However, in saying that, through some of the things we will discuss here, you will know and understand yourself more deeply and perhaps see yourself more clearly, which will support your authenticity and being comfortable in your own skin.

## Finding ways to let it go

As the song from Disney's *Frozen* says:

> *"Let it go! Let it go!*
> *Can't hold it back anymore*
> *Let it go! Let it go!*
> *Turn away and slam the door*
> *I don't care what they're going to say*
> *Let the storm rage on*
> *The cold never bothered me anyway"*

As with the fears and barriers that have been holding you back from being your authentic self, you have let them go. For you to be truly comfortable in your own skin, especially in the workplace, you need to find a way to let go of the potential judgement, the concerns of what others may say.

This is your life, your journey, your authenticity. It is time to take a stand and not to hold it back anymore.

### *You are not the label(s)*

For this one, I am going to talk specifically about the labels women are often given in the workplace and certainly labels I have encountered in my career when I have asserted myself. Labels such as:

- "Bossy"
- "Aggressive"
- "A bitch"

For your authenticity as an individual, certainly if you are a woman in the workplace, let us reframe those labels and give you a clear understanding of what they mean in reality:

- You are providing direction but not being "bossy".
- You are being firm but not being "aggressive".
- You are standing your ground and setting standards but not being "a bitch".

Remember that labels such as these are not generally labels given to men in the workplace, and if they are, there are fewer negative connotations associated with them. From my experience, nicknames or labels like that are considered badges of honour for the opposite sex and, while it is not fair, there is also no reason why you should concern yourself with these labels.

Typically, when I am in the situation where one of these labels has been linked to me, I will question it, using my humour and stakeholder-management skills to reframe it to something positive. I have already discussed the nickname 'smiling assassin' that I was given many years ago that I now proudly share and enjoy being used about me.

In the same way that I would share my opinion and assert myself in the workplace about a project or service being delivered, I will assert myself in the workplace when someone is trying to discredit me through the use of a label. Here is an example:

If I have asserted myself in a meeting with a third party where they needed to be held to account, and after the meeting I have been advised that my approach was too heavy-handed or aggressive – I would ask questions of the person providing the feedback, such as:

- "Thank you for the feedback. I would appreciate it if you could provide an example of how I could have asserted myself clearly, in a way that ensured the third party understood the severity of the matter, without appearing as 'aggressive'?"
- "OK, that is interesting, and I appreciate the feedback. I was in a meeting previously with <insert name>, who had taken a similar approach but with a raised voice. It would be great to understand how things should have been handled differently so I can adjust my approach."

I admit there is a dusting of passive aggression in the questions – this is because in the workplace I have also been told that I was not aggressive enough. It seems that there are times that no matter my approach, someone may have an opinion about it, and I cannot possibly satisfy or please everyone. Particularly as a woman in technology, I am often not measured by the same standards as my male counterparts and there is not always a middle ground for me to take.

The point here is that when it comes to you being authentic at work and the labels you may be given, you have a choice to address them, adjust your approach or ignore them. Regardless of the approach you take, it is going to be the one that is right for you. So, in that vein, who cares what the labels are? If you can hold your head high and know that you have acted in a manner that aligns with your values and is respectful, the viewpoint of others is entirely irrelevant.

I will share more about this in a few moments in the section "Finding out 'Who am I?'".

### Be the ice queen

Although I have been unable to find the origin of one of my favourite quotes, it is pertinent to share it with you now:

> *"Fate whispers to the warrior, 'You cannot withstand the storm.' The warrior whispers back, 'I am the storm.'"*

I hope that as you read this book, you pick up on my nature as a warm, kind individual whose mission in life is to support others in their journey to not only be themselves but also to succeed. I am not the embodiment of a maternal figure, nor do I want to be seen as such. There are times in the workplace where a woman who is not seen as a mother figure will be seen as cold or disengaged, when in fact she is probably just trying to get on with her job, do the best she can for herself and her team.

I baulk against the idea that because of my anatomy I should be anything other than who I am. In the same way that it should be perfectly acceptable for a man to be in touch with his emotions,[33] to empathise and to be vulnerable without any impact on his credibility or character, a woman should be able to be assertive, powerful and decisive without being considered cold-hearted or unfeeling.

Vulnerability in men, or anyone, is something that should be celebrated, not ridiculed. The point here is that men also have labels to contend with, which are unfair, unjust and restrictive.

In one of my previous roles, I was called 'The Ice Queen' because I can often disassociate and distance myself from emotive topics in the workplace (compartmentalising). I do this because in my professional capacity in an organisation, I understand that business decisions need to be made. These business decisions often need clear, holistic and objective oversight rather than an emotional response, particularly when you are in a leadership role.

Does it hurt my feelings being considered cold or icy? Yes, sometimes it does, but ultimately that viewpoint is not accurate and the people who make those statements obviously do not know me very well. From my perspective, I would rather maintain my countenance, authenticity and professionalism than appear as something more socially acceptable to others.

**Tip:**

**People's misunderstandings of you are not your responsibility to manage or correct.**

---

[33] Toxic masculinity is detrimental to society, and the whole idea of 'man up', 'grow a pair' or 'boys don't cry' is something that many men struggle with.

### *Let your inner goddess shine*

Part of 'letting it go' includes allowing yourself to be who you are, without getting bogged down by the opinions of others or what may be considered the norm. What you are doing is showing up for yourself and as yourself, without apology and allowing all your idiosyncrasies to shine.

You are the story that led you to where you are today. You do not need to hide parts of yourself to 'fit in'. Remember: perfection is an ideal, not a reality – no one is perfect. One of my favourite T-shirts that I regularly wear is a simple black one with the words 'be weird' on it. I love it.

Everyone masks in one way, shape or form, and this is OK, but at the same time, it is important to embrace your inner self, removing the need to pretend to be anything other than who you are. Your authentic energy will become magnetic, and your shine will invite curiosity, connection and inspiration from those around you.

Express yourself. Share how you feel, what you think and let your voice be heard.

### Finding your peace

Once you have found the ways that work for you to 'let it go', it is time to find out where your inner peace comes from. The inner peace may be due to having a balance and accepting awareness of yourself, it may be from finding ways to express yourself externally, or it may be a combination of the two. Whatever it is, wherever you find your peace, make a note of it and ensure you invest in and set aside time to just hang out in that space.

## *What makes YOU happy?*

One of the key things about finding your peace is investing time in activities, passions and hobbies that YOU are interested in. During our lives, it is easy to get sucked into activities and hobbies that the people around us are interested in, rather than following our own path. This could be doing things with your significant other that are not really your thing but it means spending time with them, or perhaps not taking up a new hobby because you fear your friends will judge or tease you about it. Whatever the reasons, it is for you to decide what you want to do and what interests you.

It is worth saying briefly that I am not suggesting you do not get involved in the interests of the people you care for and love. I am definitely not saying that to be in any relationship will not require an element of compromise and maybe sacrifice. What I am saying, however, is that those compromises and sacrifices should not be at the cost of who you are or of spending time doing the things that YOU love.

An example of what I mean by this is that as I am writing this sitting at my kitchen island, my partner is sitting at the kitchen table putting together a plastic model kit – something that he loves to do. I love to write and am incredibly passionate about sharing my thoughts about authenticity with you through this book, and I also love spending time with him. He loves building and painting a range of models and also loves spending time with me. Our compromise to allow each other space to do our own thing is to be in the same physical space together, each doing our own activities, creating a harmony of different interests while spending time together.

So, let me ask you the question: What makes you happy?

I do not expect you to have the answers readily at hand, because if you are anything like me, it may take a while to figure it out. It may take a while to be comfortable enough in your own skin to break away from the mould of your friends and family to actually talk about your passions. It may be that there were things you never had the opportunity to do as a child that you want to do as an adult, such as dancing, gymnastics, writing, travel, and so on.

In 2021, I saw a post from someone on Instagram, who was questioning the status quo about bikini bodies and advocating body positivity, while also embracing stepping out of your comfort zone to do something you have never tried before. I did a bit of research about this person and discovered they took up pole dancing in their forties. I was intrigued and wanted to give it a go.

Before I tell you about that journey, let me tell you briefly about a friend I had for many years whose opinion mattered greatly to me. This person was strong in their opinions of what people should and should not do, and I often found myself less likely to do things if I thought I would be at the receiving end of their judgement. I am a strong-minded individual and happy to stand out from the crowd, but I have felt like I do not fit in for much of my life, hiding parts of my personality, so at times, I have just wanted an easy life and to blend in.

At the time I was ready to try pole dancing, my friendship with this person had fizzled out, which although incredibly sad, meant that I was less concerned about how I would be perceived and more focused on the nerves of stepping out of my comfort zone to try something new, at the ripe old age of 43.

By 2025, at the time of writing this, I had learned pole dancing for 18 months, gaining strength and stamina, though perhaps not grace in my movement. I also began learning aerial hoop three and a half years ago and absolutely love it. If you have not seen aerial hoop, it is a metal hoop that is suspended from the ceiling within which you perform acrobatics, spins and strength exercises, which are both exhilarating and terrifying. Each lesson I attend has me stepping outside of my comfort zone, pushing my boundaries, facing my fears and having an absolute blast.

The studio in Huddersfield where I train, PPD Studios, is one of my happy places. All responsibilities, drama and bullshit is left in the car park. When I am there, I am with a community of supportive individuals who just see Sophie. They do not see the mum, the leader, the partner, the business owner – it is just a space for me to be me.

### *Dropping the dead weight*

There are going to be necessary evils in life that you just have to deal with. Like paying tax, going to the dentist, washing your hair when you really cannot be bothered, and so on. This is just life. However, there will be things in your life that you can remove to give you the space to breathe and allow yourself the best opportunity to be your authentic self. And ultimately be happy.

Think of this like decluttering a house, but instead you are decluttering your life for your own well-being and peace of mind.

Examples of where you could do this include the following:

- **Not giving in to negative self-talk**

  Ignore that inner voice that says you are not good enough, or you have no right to be there, or you always get things wrong. Reframe these with "I am doing my best", "Perfection is an ideal, not a reality".

- **Toxic relationships**

  It can be hard to recognise those relationships that are damaging to your mental health and well-being. There are potentially people in your network who will be barriers to you being your authentic self. Consider the people around you. It is OK to recognise those who diminish your skills, strengths, abilities. It is OK to recognise those who do not support you. It is OK to recognise those who drain, belittle or manipulate you. It is also OK to remove yourself from relationships that are in any of those categories and more. Even if they are with family members. In my experience, just being related to someone by blood does not mean that they will accept, like or support you. I have found a handful of people in my adult life whom I consider family who are not blood relatives.

- **Complaining without action**

  We all complain about and share those things that irritate us. We vent and talk about what or how things could be better. But do we also talk about the ways to resolve the issue or the solution to the problem? It is important here to ensure that when venting or complaining, you either take action to address the situation OR accept it and move on. The power here is with you. You can make a decision for the best path to take, but my advice would be not to carry with you the weight of things that piss you off.

- **People-pleasing**

I can talk about this one until the cows come home. For a variety of reasons, my go-to persona has, historically, been a people pleaser. This is something that is deeply rooted in my DNA and something that I have used the expertise of a counsellor to address.

When it comes to pleasing other people, I, of course, want to live in a world that is amicable, comfortable and as conflict-free as possible. This is my utopia. The world is not like this, and I accept that no matter what effort I put in, some people will not be pleased. So, the approach here for me is to act according to my values, treat people with respect but not overstep my boundaries purely to make others more comfortable. To do otherwise serves no purpose and is damaging to your own well-being and mental health.

- **Comparing yourself to others**

Comparison is an evil that only results in negative outcomes. In a world where 'perfect' ideals and images are shared freely, anything differing to that ideal are shamed and ridiculed, highlighting that there is little room for anything other than that ideal. But this is simply not something you can abide by and involves rules you cannot follow.

If I have said it once, I have said it a thousand times: "Perfection is an ideal, NOT a reality." If you choose only two areas to drop the dead weight, choose this one along with removing toxic relationships. Comparing yourself to others will only do you harm. It serves no purpose and will only make you unhappy.

> **Tip:**
>
> *"Comparison is the thief of joy."*
>
> **Theodore Roosevelt**

- **Environments that drain you**

    This is slightly harder when it comes to removing the dead weight, particularly if that location that you find draining is your place of work. But you can make the decision to seek alternative work and try to remove yourself from that environment. Or if that is not an option, find a way to limit the impact the environment has on you.

There are two examples of this that I can share with you from my personal experience. One was a workplace and the other is personal.

*Workplace:*

I worked for an outsourcing organisation, where I was working on a client site. It was a job that allowed me to successfully move from the south to the north of England, where I was starting an exciting new life. In the nine months

I worked there, I saw my manager twice. They were based near Birmingham, which was about an hour and a half's drive to where I was working.

My manager did not want to bother making the trip to the north to visit me, ensure I was settling in and have a conversation with me face to face. They were open about the time it took to travel to Leeds from where they were based. I was acutely aware that my colleagues who lived closer to the south were visited on a far more regular basis. When combining this lack of care and support from my line manager with the fact that I had moved 200 miles away from everything I had grown up with and everyone I knew, the isolation was oppressive.

The job I was fulfilling was interesting enough, but I was always on the periphery of what my peer group was doing. There were regular social events that I felt excluded from. The client I was working for was lovely, but I was very much the supplier working on their home turf. I did not feel comfortable at all, and I was not learning. There was no opportunity for me to grow. And very little support was available.

As luck would have it, one of the contractors who worked on the same client site as me, took a permanent role for a company five miles from where I was working and they offered me a position with them. I jumped at the chance to remove myself from an environment that was damaging to me. The move to the north was exciting but isolating while I found my place in my new world. I did not need to feel that same isolation in the workplace, so I removed myself from it.

I handed my notice in during the second time I met my manager, which was my annual review, and to which I had had to drive 100 miles to attend, but that is a different story – albeit one I am proud of for how I handled both a toxic workplace and manager.

### *Personal:*

I have mentioned learning pole dancing and that I did it for 18 months. I loved it at the outset but after about 12 months, I realised I was in an environment that I found upsetting and difficult. Let me explain why. I was in a mixed-ability class where my fellow students (who are all amazing) were levels ahead of me. They were many years my junior and had the benefit of a youthful flexibility that I just did not have. My fellow students were incredible supporters of me and would cheer me on when I achieved something that I found challenging. It was heart-warming.

But…

My instructor was less supportive and considerate. I was the only person in the room who was classed as a beginner. I was the only person in the room who was considered 'plus size'. My instructor needed to balance the lesson plan with things that were accessible but challenging for me, with things that would challenge the rest of the class. I recognise that this was not an easy lesson to plan. That being said, my instructor would give me moves to practise on repeat, from the start of the lesson, which would exhaust me in minutes.

I would be told to "just move your body like this" and shown how to move a petite frame to achieve it. There was no accounting for a larger bust, or wider hips, or the simple fact that at 43 years old, MY body just would not move in the same way as the instructor's did. I would leave the lesson totally disheartened, often crying on my way home because I felt like a failure.

I invested in private lessons with the studio owner, which were a polar opposite experience. 'Supportive', 'kind', 'inclusive' and 'confidence-boosting' are the words I would use to describe the private lessons. I even tried attending other classes taught by the other instructors who were as fantastic as the studio owner. But the damage had been done. The detrimental impact of the toxic environment of the usual lessons, despite the support from my fellow students, has resulted in me giving up pole dancing for the time being. I recognised the effect it was having on me and my mental health. The best solution was to remove myself from an environment that I found harmful. My confidence was at an all-time low, but thankfully it is now on the rise. One day, I will return to learn pole dancing again, but for now I am happy with learning just one aerial discipline – aerial hoop.

### *Having space to breathe*

There are times where you will need to step away, get some fresh air (not necessarily literally) to allow yourself to breathe. To let the weight of everyday life, the responsibilities, the challenges and fears of just being, to drop – even if for a short while. It is important to note that there is no right or wrong way to do this. Whatever you do to decompress, to pause and just be in the moment is yours to own and do.

Personally, I have three key ways that I do this:

- **Hiking/walking**

  There is something uplifting to my spirit when I see mountains and rugged countryside. I think it is because it takes me back to my childhood holidays in North Wales where my family would walk for miles and miles up and down mountains, around lakes, and explore. When I go for a walk, particularly in the more remote locations, I can literally feel the weight of my normal responsibilities slip away for a while. It is just me in that moment, drinking in my surroundings and being at peace with the world.

  I rarely think about everyday things when I am out hiking. My focus is more on "oh crap, it's another false peak" or "damn, this is steep" or "wow, that view is breathtaking". I am purely in that moment and at one with myself.

- **A trip to the seaside**

  Similar to going to a walk, going to the seaside also lifts my spirits.

  I grew up in a part of England that is one of the farthest points from the sea, so whenever we did go to the seaside in my childhood, it was a real treat. I have spent the last 25 years just outside of Halifax in West Yorkshire, which is also not near the seaside. I live relatively close to a motorway and when sitting in my garden, if I imagine really hard, I can pretend the motorway noise is the sea, too. But there is no substitute for the real thing.

When I go to the seaside, I prefer to go on days where the sky is stormy and moody. There is an atmosphere with it that my soul recognises, finding a peace and calm from less popular weather. There is the added benefit of most people typically avoiding going to the seaside on colder, wetter days, so, often, the beach is empty or practically so. This lack of other humans allows me the space to be present in the moment. Normally when I go to the seaside, I will find a quiet place to sit where I can look out to sea, watching the waves and just allowing the sounds, sights and smells of my surroundings wash over me, bathing me in a sense of peace. I often end up sitting there absorbing my surrounding for hours.

Unlike when I go for a hike or walk, I do think about what is happening in my life, and perform a sort of analysis of how I am feeling and what is going on, and I try to be objective about it all. I give myself the space to cry, to vent internally, to reflect as needed. I do not typically define a plan of action or try to solve problems, though – it is more about allowing myself the space to process what is happening in my life at that moment, aiming to accept it, ready to form a plan when I am back home or at work.

- **A bolt hole**

This last one is utterly dependent on time, money and availability. But having a place away from my normal surroundings to go to and spend a night or two just distancing myself from normal life is a relief. One of the best examples of this was during the COVID-19 pandemic, where we were allowed to create a 'bubble' with another person or family while maintaining the social distancing rules from everyone else. I live about 200 miles away from my parents and siblings (one of whom is in Canada), so creating a bubble with them was not an option. A very good friend of mine (who is now my partner) offered to create a bubble with me, which meant I could go and stay with him at his apartment on the weekends my daughters were with their father. I would finish work on the Friday, wave my children off and jump in the car to drive to his apartment. From the moment I walked into the apartment building, I could feel the weight and stress of everything I was experiencing drop from my shoulders.

I would spend the weekend sleeping on the sofa, watching films, reading books and just being in the moment. I would not really do any reflection or thinking. I would simply allow my brain to switch off for two days to be present, to be Sophie, and to allow myself adequate space to breathe. It was gloriously freeing and not something I experience as often these days. However, if the opportunity arises for a cheeky weekend retreat to somewhere near the sea, then I take the chance to go and just be at peace.

## 9: Investing in the bank of you

There are multiple options available for those who can leave their responsibilities for a while. You may want to try some of the things that work for me or find something that is better aligned to you and what would work best for you. If it is not possible to leave your responsibilities easily (e.g. caring responsibilities), you could try finding a few minutes at work or at home to close your eyes and meditate, to give yourself some headspace. Regardless of what you do or where you do it, it is important that you can find the space to catch a breath, take a break or get some respite, even if for a short while.

**Finding your passion(s)**

Our interests are part of what make us unique and are an influencing factor for being authentic. Having a hobby is often a way for us to invest time in things we are interested in and to continue to learn about our interests. The word 'hobby' can strike fear in the heart of the strongest person – with associations of 'organised fun' or the thought of having to engage in large, noisy groups of people when you are an introvert, and so on. When we talk about finding your passions and hobbies here, we are not talking about any of that, but more about making time for you to do things that you enjoy.

Some examples of hobbies and interests include:

- Painting/drawing
- Photography
- Pottery/ceramics
- Creative writing/journaling

- Digital art/animation
- Cooking or baking
- Home DIY projects
- Sewing or fashion design

- Knitting/crocheting
- Scrapbooking
- Reading
- Meditation/mindfulness
- Gardening
- Astrology/tarot
- Hiking
- Running/jogging
- Rock-climbing
- Dance (hip-hop, salsa, etc.)
- Martial arts
- Gymnastics
- Aerial arts (hoop, trapeze, silks, pole)
- Upcycling/repurposing
- Playing an instrument
- Singing/songwriting
- Amateur dramatics and acting
- Travelling
- Learning languages
- Board/table-top role playing games
- Wine- or food-tasting clubs
- Yoga or Pilates
- Roller-skating/ice-skating
- Surfing/paddleboarding
- Blogging or vlogging
- Gaming (console or PC)

Or your hobby may be none of these things, which is equally OK.

The key point here is finding something outside of the workplace that brings you joy. Somewhere you can further embrace the exploration of your authenticity, your personality and finding out who you are. To do some of these things, you may need to go it alone, further stepping outside of your comfort zone.

When I started learning pole dancing and aerial hoop, I did not know anyone at the studio and going to that first lesson, I was filled with nerves. I was not sure what the other students would be like, whether it would be a welcoming environment, etc. but I also knew I wanted to try something new. I was seriously pushing my boundaries and nowhere near comfortable, but it turned out to be one of the best decisions I have ever made. I have never been in an environment so psychologically safe, full of acceptance, love and kindness from my fellow students and everyone in the aerial arts community.

### Exploration and adventure

When talking about exploration and adventure, this could be in the typical sense of travel and outdoor activities but equally, it can mean self-exploration and the adventure of finding yourself, your passions and the journey to being your fully authentic self.

### No limits to finding your happy place(s)

There are no limits to the number of passions and interests you can have. The only potential limitations that may exist is the time you have available to invest in your hobby and perhaps the cost of equipment or lessons. But this is something you can control and decide upon. You also do not have to stick with just one or two hobbies, doing them for a long time. You can chop and change as much as you would like (taking into consideration the costs associated with stopping a hobby) – it is your prerogative.

It will come as no surprise to you that one of my happy places is at the studio, training aerial hoop. I originally started learning pole dancing and then switched, with my main focus being hoop. I have also tried trapeze, lollipop (this is a hoop on a pole that spins), silks, Cyr wheel and several others. I have not continued learning them for a variety of reasons and I am comfortable with that – happy in the knowledge that I tried.

**Finding out "Who am I?"**

When it comes to authenticity, being yourself and finding the confidence to remove those masks, it is more than a question of "who am I", it is also asking yourself "who do I want to be". In the opening chapters of this book, we spoke about the barriers to authenticity and those things that may cause you to be afraid of allowing your authentic self to shine. When you are asking yourself the question of who you are and who you want to be, you may feel that being yourself may be met with judgement or some form of backlash from others – this is perfectly natural. However, this chapter is all about **YOU**. It is not about other people, their opinions, their values, their judgement – these things need to be put to one side while you continue your journey of self-discovery and finding your power.

While writing this book, I have reconnected to music from my younger years, and the chorus of Charlotte Church's "Finding My Own Way" (*Tissues and Issues*, 2005 resonates strongly with what we are talking about here:

> *"I'm just finding my own way, in my own sweet time*
> *If I'm making a mistake at least it's mine*
> *If I travel down a different road, to the one that you would take*
> *I'm just finding my own way".*

Investing the time in understanding who you are and who you want to be is a deeply personal activity, one where you need to remove all the outside influences as much as possible. This is so you can have a clear head, or clearer vision, to really be introspective, reflective and define what makes you, you.

### What defines you?

What are the labels or roles that you hold that could be used to define who you are? For example, are you any of the following?

- A leader;
- An entrepreneur;
- A visionary;
- A solid performer;
- An introvert/extrovert/ambivert;
- A lone wolf;
- A parent;
- A fur-parent;
- A sibling;
- An only child; or
- A wife/husband/partner/girlfriend/boyfriend.

This list could continue with so many potential descriptive roles or terms.

While considering these types of descriptive terms, also throw in the various descriptive words that can be used to denote values to see which resonate with you most about who you want to be. For example, words like the following:

- Courageous

- Powerful
- Honest
- Kind-hearted
- Successful
- Determined
- Conscientious
- Ambitious
- Truthful
- Brave
- Proud
- Individualistic
- Supportive

Do any of these words call out to you and say "yes, this is who I am and how I want to be defined"? We have already spoken about defining your values and the importance they play in your journey to being authentic. Now it is time to consider how those words weave into the fabric of the person you are, and whether there are other adjectives that make up who you are.

Something that is important to talk about here when talking about labels, in the context of your authenticity, is that the term 'label' is about understanding the facets of you that make you a whole. In the wider sense, the term 'label' does not always come with positive connotations, as we have already seen. It is a salient point to consider what those labels may mean and how you feel about them.

Let me provide some more context of what I mean by this, using a personal example.

I am a woman and a mother. These are two labels that I am incredibly proud of but there are expectations of me with those two roles that do not align with who I am. Many years ago, I visited a friend who had just had a baby. It was her second child; we knew each other because our eldest children went to the same nursery (day care). Pretty much as soon as I walked through the door, she passed the newborn to me to hold (if you have read the chapter where I talk about emotional labour, you will already know that this is up there with my worst nightmares!).

It went against my upbringing to say that I did not want to hold the baby because it would feel like I was being rude. I gritted my teeth, slapped a smile on my face and went with the moment because I knew it would not be for too long. The problem I had not considered is that children pick up on the vibes in the room. The baby knew I did not want to hold them, and they started crying.

This was an "oh, for fuck's sake" moment for me. Instantly, I was even more uncomfortable than when the kid was thrust upon me. I immediately went to give the baby back to my friend because I had only just met them and had no idea how to comfort them. This is despite having children of my own.

My friend's response as she took her baby back from me was: "You have your own kids, you should know what to do." It was an unintended moment of judgement from her but one that stung a little and I did retort: "I know how to comfort my own children, but I don't know what works for yours." I did say it in as much of a light-hearted way as possible, but I was hoping the message was clear. Yes, I am a mother to my children, by choice. Just because I have this label of being 'mother' does not mean I know how to or want to placate other people's children. I would never want to see another parent struggle and am "that" person who will offer to help people in the street with carrying a pushchair up a flight of stairs, or to help a friend in need to have a break when overwhelmed. But this wasn't that – my friend just handed me the baby, without asking me or checking if I was comfortable helping them.

See, the thing here is that I am more than a parent. I am more than a partner, a sister, a family member, etc. I am more than the job titles I have held. I follow my own path. I live by my values. I am comfortable in my own skin because I am a sum of all the facets of me. I do not want to be defined by just one aspect of my life or one label that may be associated with me, because that will not give people a true picture of who I am.

I am the sum of all my parts. As are you. You are unique. And if being unique means challenging the status quo, the labels and the stereotypes, then so be it. Take the time to understand who you are, your authenticity and embrace who you are.

## Personal development is not just for the workplace

There are many people I know who are different in the workplace than they are in social situations and in their personal lives. I am one of these people, as we have discussed earlier. I am more confident at work and embrace those seemingly extroverted parts of myself in the office. I love attending the training sessions where you learn your colours, your personality types, your level of emotional intelligence, etc. This is because it is fascinating to learn about my fellow attendees, but also because what I am learning may be useful in my personal life.

The personal-development objectives that you need to define each year for your performance review at work do not need to be limited to the workplace. Some of the most successful and fully authentic people I know spend the time also defining their personal goals, setting their intentions for the year. They also follow up on those goals to see if they have achieved them, if they need to course correct. I am not afraid to admit that I have not quite managed to master this activity, but that is OK, I am still on my personal-development journey.

There are many ways to work on your personal development. It could be through self-study – there are hundreds of books and resources out there, guiding you on building confidence, assertiveness, productivity methodologies, etc. In the appendix, there are links to Simon Sinek, Brené Brown, Getting Things Done (GTD®), and Forbes's top 25 self-help books.

There is a wealth of podcasts out there, too, such as:

- High Performance podcast
- The Diary of a CEO
- Mel Robbins's podcast
- Alex Cooper presents Call Her Daddy

All covering a variety of topics with guest speakers sharing experiences that you can learn from (see the appendix for details).

We will talk about direct help you can obtain in the next section, but there are also mentors and coaches and a range of professionals who can help you with your personal development.

There are three common personal-development courses in the workplace that are useful to attend and to personally invest more time investigating:

1. Emotional intelligence
2. Insights
3. Personality types

**Emotional intelligence**

In a nutshell, emotional intelligence means the ability to recognise and notice what you are feeling in a given moment, understand why you are feeling it and respond to it in a positive, constructive way.

For example: You are driving down a road in a relatively slow line of moving traffic. The car behind you overtakes you, having not realised the queue in front and then practically performs an emergency stop just in front of you, causing you to have to do the same. You are frustrated and possibly angry at the recklessness of the other driver.

If you have low emotional intelligence, you may scream and shout at them, drive too close to them to 'show them a lesson' and be angry all day.

If you have high emotional intelligence, you may feel frustrated and briefly angry, but you then pause to take a breath, accept how you feel in that moment and move on. You are not angry all day. The impact of the incident was short-lived.

The theory behind having strong emotional intelligence is that it equates to being a better leader, having better relationships, being better at making decisions and having a more positive well-being.

Having attended an emotional intelligence training course which utilised the EQ-i 2 tool (link in the appendix), I can honestly say I found the session fascinating and left the workshops with a better understanding of not only my emotional intelligence, but also that of those around me. I attended with other leaders in the organisation I was working for, and it gave me an insight into the senior leadership team and how they led. I learned how understanding their levels of emotional intelligence would help me tailor my interactions with them to better align with how they would respond to situations, escalations, etc.

## Insights – Learning your colours

Insights is a psychometric tool that, according to Insights.com:

> *"uses a simple and memorable four colour model to help people understand their style, their strengths and the value they bring to the team. We call these the colour energies, and it's the unique mix of Fiery Red, Sunshine Yellow, Earth Green and Cool Blue energies, which determines how and why people behave the way they do."*[34]

As with the EQ-i 2 tool used by professionals to assess emotional intelligence, Insights is a very interesting tool to use to understand where your personality fits among the four colours.

It was not a form of psychometric analysis that I had come across until 2022, where my client sent all their colleagues on the course to help them understand themselves and how to collaborate with each other effectively. After

---

[34] *https://www.insights.com/.*

attending the course, colleagues in the organisation would include their colour profile in their email signature. This was to help set expectations of the people they were communicating with on how they work best.

Here is a generalised definition of what the colours mean:

- **Red** = action-oriented, proactive, makes decisions quickly
- **Yellow** = typically an extrovert, an optimist, socially dexterous, innovative
- **Green** = empathetic, people-focused, high emotional intelligence
- **Blue** = data driven, typically introverted, detail-oriented, slower to make decisions

When you complete the course, you get a complete analysis of your colour profile, which typically results in having one or two dominant colours. As with the emotional intelligence course, it is not only insightful from a personal perspective but also enlightening to find out what your colleagues, peers and leaders' colour profiles are. You can learn and understand how to better interact with people while also setting expectations of what works best for you.

One of my favourite ways to illustrate this technique is to describe how those who have red in their colour profile respond to instant messages. If someone sends a message saying "hi Sophie" and then does not provide any context for why they have messaged me, this triggers the red part of my personality. The green part of my colour profile wants to help the person and provide support, but I need them to get to the point…and quickly.

This may make you laugh, but in one organisation I worked for, I left one such message unread for three weeks. There is no exaggeration here with the timescale. The person just said "hi Sophie" and never got to the point or sent a follow-up message. I was busy and did not have time for chitchat so did not respond. Perhaps not my finest moment. This was before I understood what Insights was. Had we both been on the course, perhaps I would have learned that the other person wanted to know if I was available to talk and needed me to acknowledge their message before they could get to the point and ask their question.

## Personality types

The Myers-Briggs Type Indicator® (MBTI®) assessment[35] is one of the most commonly known tests for defining and understanding your personality type. The below is from the Myers-Briggs website and describes what it is:

*"The Myers-Briggs Type Indicator® (MBTI®) Step I is based on Carl Jung's theory of psychological type. It indicates your personality preferences in four dimensions:*

- *Where you focus your attention – Extraversion (E) or Introversion (I)*

- *The way you take in information – Sensing (S) or INtuition (N)*

---

[35] *https://www.myersbriggs.org/.*

- *How you make decisions – Thinking (T) or Feeling (F)*

- *How you deal with the world – Judging (J) or Perceiving (P)"*

It is an assessment that goes back to the mid-20th century and is used in many organisations globally.

The first time I did this assessment in the workplace was in around 2012. All the people managers in the organisation were sent on a course to support their understanding of themselves as well as those around them. What was particularly interesting to me about the whole assessment, was that I have a duality between my natural introvert and displaying extrovert tendencies in the workplace.

Before completing the prerequisite questionnaire, I asked the instructors how I should answer the questions about "Sophie at work" or "Sophie at home", because the outcome may differ. They were a little surprised at the question and suggested that I should answer in a work context. I answered using my instinct and from the workplace perspective, which resulted in not fully agreeing with the outcome. The first letter in my MBTI result was an **E,** which signified that I am an extrovert – which I am most definitely not. I may potentially be an ambivert, but this was not something widely discussed as a 'thing' when I took the course.

As with the EQ-i 2 tool and Insights tool results, understanding your personality type and that of those around you is enlightening. It can help you understand yourself better and how to more effectively collaborate with your colleagues.

## No one wants to be typecast

I have already mentioned the William Shakespeare quote about being a 'jack of all trades', which is often shortened to have a negative meaning. Whereas, in fact, the quote is about the benefits of being a generalist or having multiple specialities.

Let us bring this to life using an example. If you think of the leading character from Star Wars®, Luke Skywalker, you will most likely imagine the face of the actor, Mark Hamill. After the resounding success of the Star Wars franchise, Mark Hamill has appeared in other films. But he is typecast in the role of Luke Skywalker as his most successful years as an actor have been in those roles. Or let us talk about female actors who have been in a long line of romantic comedies. They often find it hard to break into the more dramatic roles and step away from the comedic characters they are most associated with.

When it comes to your authenticity, you need to decide how you want to be seen. Do you want to be seen as one thing, or many? What parts of your authenticity are the ones you want to be known for?

## Finding your personal Yoda[36]

In all of this, you do not have to fly solo and take this journey alone. Yes, your authenticity is yours to find, own and personify, but there are times where you need advice, guidance and support from others. The length of time you

---

[36] Yoda is a fictional character from the Star Wars franchise. He is a humanoid alien who offers words of wisdom and council to characters he interacts with.

need or want for additional support is entirely up to you, but there are options available to you such as:

- Mentoring;
- Coaching; and
- Communities (of practice, of support, of like-minded individuals).

From a mental-health perspective, there are also therapists, counsellors, psychologists, life coaches, and so on.

### *Mentoring*

Having a mentor is like having your own personal tour guide.

A mentor is someone whom you speak to on a regular basis to gain insight into a variety of scenarios based on their experience and knowledge. They are someone who can help you navigate your own path (typically with a work life focus, but can also support you in your personal life) with confidence, direction and a level of objectivity. In my experience, mentors typically offer their support for free although there are some who are paid for their mentorship services. Here is what you get out of the relationship:

- **Guidance from experience**

  Mentors have 'been there, done that', they have made mistakes, got it wrong and figured it out. It is like learning the shortcuts through IKEA without having to find a map or walk through the store a thousand times to learn the secret paths.

- **Personalised feedback**

Your mentor wants you to succeed, grow and thrive. They will give you feedback that comes from a place of knowing you and wanting to support you on your journey. The feedback will be honest, not always comfortable, but will give you insight into what to work on/from.

- **Accountability**

  Your mentor will listen to you and what is happening and give you their honest opinion, which will include holding you accountable when perhaps you need some perspective or objectivity. They will also help you stay on track and accountable for your development – they are giving up their time to support you.

- **Encouragement, confidence boosts and emotional support**

  Having someone there who can say, "it's OK", "it will work out", "I'm here for you, how can I help", "you've got this" or "yes, it's a bit shit, but it's a learning journey that you can handle" is an incredibly powerful thing. Your mentor is in your corner, giving you the boosts and pushes you need to continue your journey.

- **30,000ft view**

  When you are feeling overwhelmed or caught in the weeds, your mentor can help you take a step back to observe the bigger picture. Helping you find patterns and guiding you towards solutions that work for you.

- **Connections and resources**

  On top of all this, your mentor is likely to have a wide network of connections, resources and opportunities that you can take advantage of – ones that would not necessarily have been as easy to find on your own.

A mentor will also learn from you as much as you are learning from them – it is a mutually beneficial relationship, a two-way street.

There are many ways to find a mentor, including schemes in the workplace, programmes in the wider community, etc. There are links to some of these in the appendix (as well as links to help you research coaching, which we cover in the next section). You may you already know someone who inspires you, whose experience and knowledge are a source of interest to you – you could approach them and ask them to be your mentor! The worst thing they can do is say "no", but as we have already spoken about, you could reframe this and consider that perhaps they will say "yes". So, be brave and ask them!

I have been a mentor for about 20 years in one form or another. During my time as mentor, I have been involved in workplace schemes as well as ones in the wider technology community. I have also been honoured a few times by people approaching me and asking if I would be willing to mentor them.

I have also asked someone to be my mentor in the past. I wanted to ask someone in the senior leadership team in one of my previous roles, and there was one person who I thought was a great leader, who was direct, did not seem to get drawn in the typical office politics and whose approach I wanted to learn from. I was scared to ask but I also knew that without trying, I would never know. The person was surprised to have been asked but agreed. Over the course of about a year, we had a number of sessions where I learned a lot and it helped me continue on my personal journey both from a career perspective but also in terms of finding my comfort zone to be fully authentic at work.

## *Coaching*

Having a coach is like having your own personal magic mirror. Coaching is different from mentoring where you are typically drawing parallels from someone else's experience. It is like being centre stage, house lights down, with the spotlight shining on you with the aim to help you move forwards, working towards your goals and objectives with purpose and conviction. You can have a coach for your work or personal life, or both at once.

While there are similarities in the benefits of coaching to those of mentoring, coaching is different. Here is how:

- **Clarity and understanding**

  You get a clear picture of what you really want, versus what you think you should want. Cutting through some of the bullshit. Identifying what is in your way and addressing what matters to you. Coaches are skilled at asking you the questions that allow you to draw your own conclusions without giving you all the answers.

- **Accountability**

  You have gone to a coach because you want to make changes in some or multiple aspects of your life. We have all been in the situation where a particular idea never really left the ground because we did not follow through to achieve it. A coach will help you follow through, checking in with you, tracking your progress and holding you to account when necessary.

- **Raising your self-awareness**

There are times when we face a mental block, or we tell ourselves stories that prevent us from progressing and achieving our goals. Some of us may also self-sabotage. Your coach will help identify these patterns and behaviours so you can adjust your course to push through or past them.

- **Encouragement, confidence boosts and empowerment**

If you have ever spoken to someone who is a coach, you will know that you are working with someone special. There is a light, a drive, a power behind them or glowing from within them that will not only inspire you but also may rub off on you, too. Their perspective is likely to open your eyes to how you view things, introducing a different way to see both yourself and what you are working to achieve.

- **Tools and strategies**

To become a coach requires an investment in time, attaining qualifications and logging hours and hours of time coaching others. In the time they spend learning how to become a coach, they will be learning frameworks, tools, strategies and a variety of practical approaches to help their coachees forge a path ahead, with intention.

- **A focused, safe space**

  If you are working with a coach, then you have invested time and potentially money into dedicated slots with them. During the time spent with your coach, their focus is entirely on you, and what you are working to achieve – all in a psychologically safe space.

I have a few friends who have qualified as a coach, and I am always in awe of them and their skills. There is a light and brightness in them that draws me to them and ignites my curiosity. One of these friends has a company called Light Spark Group, which is a fantastic name that aptly captures both her personality but also all the things she offers as a coach. Another of these friends is based in Sweden – we met seven years ago when working for the same company and hit it off straight away. During our regular 'virtual drinks' catch-ups, I am always learning from her and her approach to her own development, where we speak about journalling, setting intentions and the variety of approaches and tactics she employs to support her journey.

I have not generally had masses of experience with coaches besides my friends and the typically unqualified coaching that happens in the workplace, however, about 12 months ago, I felt I needed some help and had been advised to speak with a coach. Here is the 'why':

I have never felt as though I have had a true understanding of my style when it comes to what I am wearing, particularly in the workplace. I know how to dress professionally, and I can put outfits together, but my sense of style has often felt like I just have no idea what I am doing and, often, there is a lack of confidence that goes with it. This may go back to my childhood, where we did not have much money, and often my clothes came from a church jumble sale or were hand-me-downs from my brother or other branches of the family. As an adult, I often look to my friends and colleagues for ideas and inspiration for what to wear, but again, finding something that truly worked for me felt elusive.

The person I spoke with is a friend of a friend, who works as a personal stylist. They regularly post on LinkedIn and Instagram with content that I find inspiring and uplifting. But not only that, they are unapologetically themselves, an embodiment of authenticity that I both respect and strive to be.

I reached out and scheduled an introductory session to see what they do and if they could help me. I was instantly drawn to their approach and was amazed at how quickly they made me feel at ease. The style of questioning was impressive and coach-like, probing to understand and to ensure they could help me on my journey. The follow-up session was more in-depth than the introductory session, and when the hour was up, I was incredibly hopeful that the outcome was going to bring the results I had been hoping for.

The lookbook/mood board that was created for me left me speechless. Not only did it contain a plethora of options and thinking points for me, but I was amazed at how much of me, my confidence challenges, and other aspects of my personality, had been understood in just an hour and a half. I had already left the sessions feeling more empowered, but then after seeing the information sent for me to work from, it took me to a whole other level of empowerment and confidence.

I am not wholly transformed into a fully confident person in what I wear at work, but I am a lot closer to where I want to be and from such a short amount of time. This is definitely something I am going to invest more time in going forwards.

### *Communities*

Coaching and mentoring are typically for an individual, although there are group mentoring and coaching opportunities out there. There are other sources of support and advice such as communities of practice or interest – this could be a women in technology group, a service management group, or any other type of group that brings together people with a common interest. They provide a platform or space for people to discuss, share and support one another.

When it comes to finding a community that supports your authenticity journey, it is important that you research the group and the conversations they engage in to ensure it is an appropriate space for you. The key here, when joining a community, is understanding what you are going to get from it as well as what you are going to be putting into it – it needs to be a group that aligns with your values and your mission to be your authentic self.

# CHAPTER 10: BRING FORTH THE EVOLUTION

> Focusing on personal development and growth. Being authentic means you will naturally change over time, so how do you manage that and maintain the momentum you have gained?
>
> Tackling people's reactions of "you've changed" and outgrowing friends/colleagues, especially when career success comes with resentment.

## There may be bumps in the road

It has been said a few times already in this book, but it is important to say it again…

> Perfection is an ideal, NOT a reality.

Your journey is not going to be quick, simple or easy. There are going to be times where you are trying your hardest to be yourself but the barriers in front of you seem insurmountable. This is perfectly normal and it is OK to be daunted by the troughs in the journey. The important point here is that you dust yourself off, be your own cheerleader and carry on the journey. If you analyse and assess ways to break those barriers, then you can progress.

During my time as a consultant, I have worked for a variety of clients, delivering different requirements for each. It typically takes me a few weeks to figure out how they will respond to my full authentic self before I unleash the full Sophie. In those first few weeks, I use my stakeholder-management skills to build rapport with people, to see if I can understand the boundaries and what is going to work best in their environment. All the while, I am conscious of my position as an external party, so it is important that I always act respectfully and professionally.

Due to the method of engagement through statements of work with clients, I do not expect to be considered part of the team nor to get recognition in the same way as an individual employed by the company. I also would not assert myself to act in a managerial way or overstep the boundaries of what I am there to deliver, without express permission from my client. I may offer suggestions of additional support I can provide or alternative solutions to the ones they are working on, but only directly with my key stakeholder and not their wider team, as that would be inappropriate.

During one engagement, there was a key stakeholder whom I could not seem to build solid rapport with. There were times we when we would get on brilliantly and have a laugh, and other times where there was a distinct lack of engagement or conversation from this person, coupled with a disinterested tone and body language. I often felt dismissed, undervalued and that I was being reminded of the pecking order and hierarchy in the engagement. Where I had initially thought I could be my authentic self during the contract, I found myself retreating into a previous version of me where I did not voice my opinions or offer suggestions as I would typically do. I became smaller and allowed my authenticity to be diminished in that engagement.

As the engagement progressed, my confidence also began to take a hit. Imposter syndrome was banging at my door on a daily basis. It began impacting my view of myself in a way that had me being quieter, more shy, and more introverted in settings where I had not been like that before. It was not a nice place to be. I had not been in a situation like this for many years and it was the first time as an independent consultant where I had not been able to build a good relationship with the people I was working with.

When the engagement ended, I felt a flood of relief wash over me. I was out of what I felt to be a toxic environment for me, but I was not instantly OK. I did not immediately feel as though I could embrace my authentic self at work. There was a significant amount of masking in my following engagements while I worked on rebuilding.

Now, though, several engagements later, I have regained my confidence and feel able to embrace my authentic self in the workplace again. I invested time in myself to reflect on what had happened, how it made me feel, how that correlated with my values, and so on. I also gave myself the space to just be. In the events I attended, I engaged with other consultants and asked if they had had similar experiences, how they dealt with it and to seek their advice.

I also know now what the signs are when something is not working for me. Although, I have not necessarily learned how to address it with the stakeholder, as the dynamic between consultant and client is something I am still learning to manage in the most effective way, while still reigning true to myself and being authentic in the workplace.

**Not everyone will be on the journey with you**

In my experience, there are people who travel with you during parts of your life, but not necessarily there for the whole journey. During the time they are on your journey with you, they may be your biggest advocates and cheerleaders. My mum would say "some friends are just friends for a season" when I would talk about not having a tribe of friends from an early age that would see me throughout my life.

As we grow and evolve as adults, our values may change, along with our interests and who we are as individuals. The people around us may not evolve and grow with us – you may each adapt to the changes in each other, or it may be that relationships fizzle out. This is not always an easy fact to accept, especially when those relationships had a seemingly strong foundation.

When I was 15, I had a 'best friend' who was (and is) one of the best humans I know. She accepted me for who I was. I was completely myself with her, 100% authentic. It was a glorious few years where we were practically inseparable and had the best time together. When we ended up going to different colleges and universities, I found it hard to find a friendship that was equal to the one I had in my mid-teens. I had met some really nice people, but no one that I could be truly myself with, or at least not be 100% authentic with – perhaps 85% if I was lucky.

After finishing university and entering the world of work, the same pattern with friendships repeated itself for a number of years until I moved to the north of England. Moving 200 miles away from my family and the small group of friends I had was an easy decision for me; I had always wanted to spread my wings and step away from the comfort (or what felt like shackles at times) of the town I grew up in. In fact, I have always wanted to live overseas, an aspiration I still have but have not quite managed to achieve…yet. As easy a decision as it was to move, it was one of the most challenging times in my life.

I have always been good at connecting with people; however, my natural shyness is often a barrier. It is a barrier because I do not want to thrust myself onto others. I do not want to assume that they want to be friends beyond work or wherever I have met them. The best illustration of this is being part of a group conversation, and the conversation leads to discussing an upcoming social event. I cannot bring myself to say things like "oh, that sounds like fun, would it be OK if I came too". When I say I cannot bring myself to say it, I mean that I physically cannot get those words out of my mouth – my body and face will refuse. I cannot utter anything that would be inviting myself to an event that I have not actually been invited to.

Thankfully, I made a couple of really good friends in the first year after the move whom I was comfortable being myself around. Still maybe not 100% authentic, but very, very close.

Over the years, I have made more friends from my different jobs and hobbies where I am my authentic self, unfiltered and unapologetically so – particularly in the last three to five years. My experiences, my values and who I am as an individual have evolved to a point where I am confident in my ability to be truly myself. I accept those around me for who they are without judgement, without question and with open arms. I believe in many cases it is our differences that builds a stronger understanding and connection with the people around us, particularly when you spend the time being curious and understanding the people you love (friends, family, etc.).

The friendship group I have now does not consist of all the friends I made when originally moving to Yorkshire. It is a smaller group than you would think. Not everyone knows each other and not everyone lives close to me or even in the UK. My friendship group spans the globe – it is just harder to quickly visit some of my friends because they are in

Sweden, Finland, Spain, France and America. Not everyone has been on the full journey with me; some friends have been for a season or a few seasons. This has been hard to accept and is still a development area for me, partly because I am fiercely loyal to people I care about and see them more as family than some of my blood relatives.

I accept that I have changed over the years, and I also accept that not everyone has changed with me. In some cases, our differences are so vast that we cannot bridge the gap for a stronger, deeper understanding of one another. In other cases, our values are no longer aligned, and we have drifted apart. It is sad but it is also how life goes sometimes. Not everyone will be on your journey with you. As you evolve, it is possible that not everyone will be welcoming and accepting of your authentic self.

While I am talking about your personal network here – your friends, your loved ones, etc. – it also applies to the people you work with. I have experienced people not being on my authenticity journey in the workplace, too. But the personal side of my longer journey to be unapologetically Sophie, has had a bigger impact emotionally to overcome. This may not happen to you, and I hope for you that it does not as it is upsetting, but if it does, please remember that sometimes friends are just for a season and that is OK.

**Success and achievement may come at a price**

What 'success' looks like will be as different for each person as what 'professionalism' looks like. Being your authentic self, unashamedly and unapologetically is a mark of success in my opinion. It is a personal achievement that is not to be scoffed at. It is something to admire, inspire and aspire towards. When combining this success of being authentic at work with achievement in the workplace, it is not always met with open arms.

In the same way that not everybody will be on the journey with you, not everyone will be welcoming and supportive of your achievements. While this is frustrating, it is a fact of life and further demonstrates the point that life is not always fair. There will be times when you have worked incredibly hard to attain a specific role or achieve an objective, and there is little or no recognition from around you, or from those who are supposed to be in your corner.

In chapter 5 we talked about thunder-stealers and those people who take credit for your work. But what about those people who refuse to acknowledge your success or achievements? Recognition in the workplace is vital to anyone's growth. It is an acknowledgement of a job well done and affirmation for the person who did it. The absence of recognition can be damaging to both employee and company in terms of the following:

- Productivity
- Well-being
- Loyalty
- Overall experience

And, of course, it could potentially impact future deliverables and achievements. Recognition in the workplace goes hand in hand with the delivery of value. If you starve a cow of food, it will fail to produce milk. If you starve an employee of recognition, or even just feedback, that employee is likely to deliver less and less value over time because they may see no point in doing so. Their efforts may seem fruitless and pointless to them.

It is important to note that there is a difference between a participation award and true recognition or feedback for a job well done. Distinguishing between the two is essential to allow the receiver of the recognition to know when they are being acknowledged for being part of the wider achievement, compared to when they deserve a special mention.

Focusing a little closer on when the success of an achievement may come at a cost links back to what we have discussed earlier: you do not go to work to make friends. Sometimes, your own achievements and authenticity may unintentionally alienate the people around you. It is a fact that you need to be aware of and certainly take into account when you are spending the time to assess who you are and investing in the bank of you (chapter 9).

When I was setting up a service management function in an organisation, I began as the only person in the team besides my line manager. My line manager at the time had a wider remit than service management, so their time was not wholly focused on what I was there to deliver, as is often the way. We recruited an additional member to the team to help support me to achieve the objective to install a grounded, compliant service management framework and bring our fellow technology colleagues along on the journey.

A few years on, I was heading up the service management function and the team had grown to allow us to fulfil the vision and maintain the service standards we aimed to achieve. It was an exciting time to lead and be part of the team. We made positive waves across the department, driving change and collaborating effectively across the entire organisation. We had built a solid reputation and associated brand of who we were, setting expectations with our stakeholders, while also adapting and growing with the business as needed.

The member of the team who had been the newest recruit from a few years before was a valued member of the team, but over time their engagement and support, especially in meetings, began to wane. It became increasingly apparent that there was a negativity associated with them, and they became a disruptor, and not in a positive way. Comments made and actions taken by them were not to question the status quo or to drive continual improvement, but more to negate the direction of travel I had set, and to question the authority from which I was making decisions. They became a person who bred discontent, causing conflict within the team.

I made allowances for the person because of how long we had worked together and how much they had been part of the journey to evolve the service management team from a team of two to a team of nearly 20. I was blinkered in my objectivity and did not manage the situation, nor the individual, as well as I could have done. It was a lesson I was learning but had not realised at the time.

I cannot say what the motives were of this person, but I do know what happened in terms of impact to the wider team. There were elements of infighting, discontent, conflict and a confusion in terms of the direction we were taking and whose authority to respond to. I also cannot say if my own achievements and promotions had prompted their negativity or dimmed their view of how we were building service management across the organisation. I do have an opinion on it, but that is not relevant here.

The experience changed me forever as a people manager. While I thought I had been authentic and had been aligned to my values through this period of my career, upon reflection, I now know that was not strictly true. I was myself, but I also wanted to make sure everyone got along and that the team was 'happy'. Through the experience, I had the sharp reminder that you cannot make everyone happy, and you also cannot expect the people around you to be supportive of your success.

When I look back at this period of my career, it does make me sad. The individual and I no longer work together and what semblance of a friendship we had, no longer exists. But as we said in the previous section, not everyone is going to be on the full journey with you. It may not be fair, it may be sad or upsetting, but it is a fact of life.

Beyond my own personal experience, something I have seen of late on social media is from a couple of individuals who are wonderfully authentic and successful. They have each, and separately, posted of people in their wider networks taking their content and trying to pass it off as their own. Whoever is stealing (and I mean stealing) their content and intellectual property will not be doing it because they admire and are inspired by the original posters. They will be doing it because they are envious or jealous of the success of others, and as such are trying to take some of the limelight for themselves.

This is something for you to be aware of. Why? Because your version of authenticity may incite a response from people around you that is not always positive. Jealousy (the green-eyed monster) is not a positive bedfellow. The actions and comments made may be upsetting, frustrating or downright disappointing. As with the thunder-stealers, it is crucial for you to remember that you cannot control the actions of others. What you can control is your actions, your responses, how you maintain your authenticity, your values, and so on. Rise above it.

## Are we there yet?

When it comes to being authentic, in the workplace or generally, the questions you need to ask yourself are:

- Am I done?
- Am I the finished article?
- Is there opportunity for me to grow more?
- What if I change through experience?
- What is next for me?

Strap yourself in, I promise not to get too deep into the world of technology, but I am going to make reference to a process from the service management world that I work in, to bring this to life a little bit more.

In ITIL®, which is a framework guiding technology departments on how to best implement governance and process, there is a process for continual improvement. The purpose of it is to get to your end goal or objective and then consider whether it is working as expected, whether there are any opportunities to refine it and make it better. This process can be used in all walks of life and is not just for IT departments.

There are six questions that you ask yourself in the process:

1. What is the vision?
2. Where are we now?
3. Where do we want to be?
4. How do we get there?
5. Did we get there?

6. How do we keep the momentum going?[37]

What does it look like if you apply these questions to your journey of authenticity? Here is an example of how you could answer the questions and support yourself on your journey:

- **What is my vision?**

  To be my authentic self at work, 100% of the time.

- **Where am I now?**

  I am myself at home and with my friends but at work it is hit and miss. I do not feel like I am being truly authentic 100% of the time. I am worried about how people will react to me if I do.

- **Where do I want to be?**

  I want to be my authentic self in the workplace, be comfortable in my own skin and work somewhere that accepts and embraces individuality.

- **How do I get there?**

  I need to understand and define my values. I need to spend time understanding what my authentic self in the workplace looks like. I need to understand what holds me back and any other barriers I can perceive that may stall my journey.

---

[37] *ITIL® Foundation ITIL 4 Edition*, Axelos Global Best Practice (now PeopleCert) 2019.

- **Did I get there?**

  I am about 80% authentic at work. I have defined my values and am happy with how they reflect who I am. I am still struggling with some of the barriers to be myself, particularly imposter syndrome as it keeps raising its ugly head. There is some emotional labour in the workplace that needs to be addressed and pushed past.

- **How do I keep the momentum of my authenticity going?**

  I will keep investing the time in myself, understanding the barriers before me and how I can overcome them. I will continue to advocate for myself and my authenticity. And I will go back to the first question and continually go through this cycle.

The continual-improvement process is a cycle. In the same way that you do not just define your values once and you are done, it is something that you need to keep checking in on, keep progressing and evolving.

Your experiences in the workplace and in your personal life, along with your passions and interests, will grow and evolve over time. Therefore, it makes sense that what makes up the authentic you, will also adapt and evolve over time. The key is to ensure you stay true to your values, your path and who you are.

# CHAPTER 11: BE BOLD. BE BRAVE. BE YOU!

> **Lessons learned, pitfalls to avoid, but embracing who you are to be bold, be brave and be you.**

We are here – the final chapter – and to some extent, we are going to cover things we have already discussed in the preceding chapters.

On our journey through this book, we have spent time discussing practical tips that you can adapt and use to help you on your journey to being the authentic you that you want to be. We have spoken about:

- How your values are the cornerstones of your authenticity, and why investing time to define them is a fundamental activity for your journey to be you;
- What barriers exist for everyone in the workplace, and what specific barriers may exist for women or minority groups;
- What scares you and what may be a limiting factor, stopping you from you being who you are;
- The power of influence, in a positive sense, and using it to support you on your journey;
- Real-world examples of breaking down the barriers, both when it has worked and when it has not;
- Investing in the bank of YOU, and the importance for you to understand the 'why', creating space and embracing you; and

- How it is not 'once and done' – your journey may be bumpy and involves reflecting, investing and continually driving yourself to be authentic.

Now it is time for me to call you to action. To do this I am going to use one of my favourite sayings, which you will often see used in my social media posts:

**Be bold. Be brave. Be YOU!**

I am not entirely sure when I started using the expression, but it came about when I was trying to describe what it takes to be authentic and to phrase a mantra that could be repeated to remind oneself of what you are trying to achieve.

What does the saying mean in relation to being authentic? Let us spend some time walking through it and perhaps it will have the same meaning for you as it does for me.

**Be bold**

Being bold can take so many forms – the meaning of 'bold' is defined by you. Here are some examples:

As we have discussed and you have already learned about me, I am an introvert (or possibly an ambivert), so there are times when I have just wanted to blend into the background and get on with things without any fuss or attention in my direction. Particularly, this comes out in social situations or networking events where I have to really combat my natural shyness – specifically if the situation is one where most people know each other (or appear to) and I feel like an outsider or interloper. In these circumstances, my version of bold is to push myself beyond my comfort zone to talk to people and say hello. An example of this was just before Christmas 2024, where I had been invited to a networking event in London – I knew two people in the room of about 50 and those two people seemed to know most of the others present. I had to strap on my brave pants to get involved in conversations and put myself out there. I felt horribly uncomfortable. The sweat was real. I do not believe I came across as shy or nervous but, oh my, did I feel it! However, I survived, and it was another step in the direction of being bold.

For me, being bold is allowing yourself to shine and stand out from the crowd. You do not have to do this in a 'look at me' way that makes you the centre of attention – unless you want to, of course. You can be bold through the work you deliver, the contributions you make during meetings, how you lead by example for your team and your peers, what you wear and an air of confidence you portray (even if you are not quite there internally with the confidence).

There is immense power in standing up and elevating yourself to stand out from the norm to be your authentic self. Being bold means taking the risk and being your authentic self in all situations in spite of the fear of judgement or any of the other barriers we have previously discussed. Do it anyway!

**Be brave**

As with being bold, the meaning of what makes someone brave or courageous is defined by YOU. Not by society, not by those around you or anyone else.

The Oxford Languages and Google[38] definition of **brave** is *"ready to face and endure danger or pain; showing courage".*

The dictionary definition of **courage**, from the same source, is *"the ability to do something that frightens one".*

What frightens you may be completely different to what strikes fear in the person next to you. So, bravery and courage will differ from person to person.

Being a woman and having felt the pressure from society throughout my life, one of the ways I show bravery is to wear something I am comfortable in, that may not fit the ideals of others. This could be wearing my Toothless (from *How to Train Your Dragon* fame) hoodie to work – it is showing a part of me that could be classed as geeky with a childish aspect, but I love it; it is comfy and I feel confident when I wear it. The same goes for wearing a dress or skirt that is outside of my comfort zone, or wearing something brightly coloured in winter when people normally wear muted colours.

Another way I believe I show courage, is through not accepting poor behaviour towards me in the workplace. We have discussed the broken-record approach when someone talks over me – sometimes I have had to do this to someone senior or my line manager, but it was needs-must situation. I will always be respectful of others; however, I have no qualms highlighting that I had not finished speaking and had more to add. I have not always been brave enough to do this as it has taken time, and I have had to learn how to be my own champion in rooms where there are none.

---

[38] *https://languages.oup.com/google-dictionary-en/.*

Remember what we discussed in chapter 5 – "What are you afraid of?". Understanding what fears you have that stop you from being authentic – to fight the fear, you need to know what you are afraid of and why, so you can knock that fear to one side and embrace your authenticity.

## Be YOU!

And the final part of the saying is to be you.

We only have one go at living (depending on your beliefs), so why waste your time living under the shadow of what is 'expected' or what the 'norm' is? Embracing your personality, your beliefs, your goals and objectives, your passions, etc. is vital to your existence. Following the crowd or bending to the will of others is not likely to result in fulfilment, achievement or a sense of self.

It can be hard to shake those shackles off and break from whatever the convention is that does not fully align with who you are, and it certainly is not something that just magically happens. It takes work, time, self-reflection and development to be the unicorn or butterfly that you are.

It is OK if you do not get there at the first time trying, or even the 21$^{st}$ time – the point is to find that inner strength, that confidence and belief that being your true, authentic self is the way you want to be and the way you want to live.

Not everyone will like you.

Not everyone will respond positively to assertion, bravery and boldness.

You are not living someone else's life; you are living your own. Remember this.

You do not need to apologise for being yourself. Or for having differing opinions or values.

You do not owe anyone the right to hold you back.

You do not have to follow the advice of other people. Do your own homework and make the decision that is right for YOU.

So long as you treat people with kindness and empathy, you are on the right path.

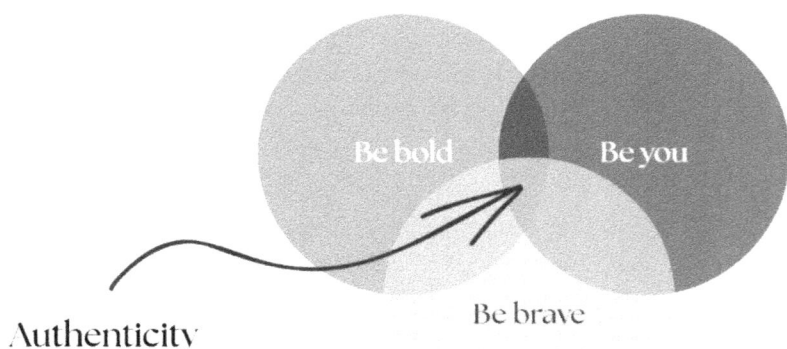

**Be bold**

**Be you**

Authenticity

Be brave

**Figure 18: The Sweet Spot**

Individually, these traits are powerful, but where they overlap, that's where authenticity lives. Boldness speaks your truth, bravery lets you stand in it and being unapologetically you brings it all to life. True authenticity isn't one thing, it's the fearless fusion of all three.

In that sweet spot – where bold meets brave meets you – you stop performing and start thriving. That's not just confidence. That's clarity. That's power. That's the real you, fully seen.

## Now it is over to you

Look how far we have come in this book, at all the things we have learned and discussed!

It is now time for you to put your own strategy into action. If you want to be truly authentic in the workplace, now is the time for you to stand tall, set your intentions and plan your journey. If you are already on the train to authenticity, consider the various topics we have discussed and spend the time to understand how this will help you continue on to your destination.

Your journey is your own. Of course, look around you for support, encouragement and inspiration on the way. The experience and advice from others can be a game-changer between being 80% authentic and 100% authentic. Reaping the benefits of advice and support from the people around you will not negate your own achievements, nor should it stray you from your path.

My daughter sent me a quote from X that strikes true here:

> *"The best part of being authentic is that there is no image to maintain. You will delight and disturb others, and none of it will concern the truth of your being."*[39]

Now is your time to take that leap. To back yourself. To be unapologetically you.

---

[39] X account @SoledadFrancis, Soledad Francis PhD, 28 April 2022.

*11: Be bold. Be brave. Be you!*

You have got this.[40]

---

[40] You can let me know how you get on and how your journey is progressing by emailing me: *authenticity@dramaticallyhonest.com*.

# APPENDIX: SOURCES, RESOURCES AND WHERE TO FIND SUPPORT

## Chapter 2: Barriers to authenticity

- *Fear of rejection*
  - Medical News Today – "Fear of rejection: What it is and how to overcome it": *https://www.medicalnewstoday.com/articles/fear-of-rejection*.
  - Psychology Today – "5 Reasons Why Social Pain Is Real": *https://www.psychologytoday.com/us/blog/the-modern-heart/201906/5-reasons-why-social-pain-is-real*.
  - NeuroscienceNews.com – "Understanding and Reframing the Fear of Rejection": *https://neurosciencenews.com/rejection-fear-20892/*.
- *Social conditioning, cultural or societal pressures and expectations*
  - NOW.org – "The Pink Tax: The Cost of Being a Woman": *https://now.org/blog/the-pink-tax-the-cost-of-being-a-woman/*.
  - The co-operative bank – "Pink Tax: Women are paying 40% more for their essentials": *https://www.co-operativebank.co.uk/content-hub/articles-and-advice/pink-tax-women-paying-more-for-their-essentials/*.

- UK Parliament – "Pink Tax": *https://edm.parliament.uk/early-day-motion/55690/pink-tax*.
- **Mental-health challenges**
  - Mind: *https://www.mind.org.uk/*.
  - Samaritans: *https://www.samaritans.org/how-we-can-help/contact-samaritan/*.
  - ANDYSMANCLUB: *https://andysmanclub.co.uk/*.
  - World Health Organization: *https://www.who.int/health-topics/mental-health*.

## Chapter 3: Barriers for women in the workplace

- **Gender bias and stereotyping**
  - Cambridge dictionary definition: *https://dictionary.cambridge.org/dictionary/english/gender-bias*.
- **Under-representation and perceptions of leadership**
  - GrantThornton – "Women in tech: A pathway to gender balance in top tech roles": *https://www.grantthornton.global/en/insights/women-in-business/women-in-tech-a-pathway-to-gender-balance-in-top-tech-roles/*.
- **Workplace inequality**
  - Office for National Statistics – "Gender pay gap in the UK: 2024": *https://www.ons.gov.uk/employmentandlabourmarket/peopleinwork/earningsandworkinghours/bulletins/genderpaygapintheuk/2024*.

- o CIO.com – "Women in tech statistics: The hard truths of an uphill battle": *https://www.cio.com/article/201905/women-in-tech-statistics-the-hard-truths-of-an-uphill-battle.html.*
- o CIO.com – "How the UK tech industry is failing Black women": *How the UK tech industry is failing Black women | CIO.*
- o McKinsey & Company – "Women in the Workplace": *https://wiw-report.s3.amazonaws.com/Women_in_the_Workplace_2022.pdf.*
- **Imposter syndrome**
  - o Harvard Business School – "Breaking Through the Self-Doubt That Keeps Talented Women from Leading": *https://www.library.hbs.edu/working-knowledge/breaking-through-the-self-doubt-that-keeps-talented-women-from-leading.*
  - o KPMG – "Advancing the Future of Women in Business": *https://assets.kpmg.com/content/dam/kpmg/sk/pdf/2020/2020-KPMG-Womens-Leadership-Summit-Report.pdf.*
- **Sexual harassment and discrimination**
  - o *Allyship Actually: https://allyshipactually.com/.*
- **Balancing professionalism and femininity**
  - o sghworldwide – "The first computer designed just for women – The Petticoat 5 $5000"*: https://www.youtube.com/watch?v=iVquI-MVmd0.*

    o Channel 4's *The IT Crowd*:
   *https://www.channel4.com/programmes/the-it-crowd*.

## Chapter 4: What are your values

- Mind Tools – "What Are Your Values?":
  *https://www.mindtools.com/a5eygum/what-are-your-values*.
- Brené Brown: "Dare to Lead: List of Values":
  *https://brenebrown.com/resources/dare-to-lead-list-of-values/*.
- BetterUp: Personal values examples:
  *https://www.betterup.com/blog/personal-values-examples*.

## Chapter 5: What are you afraid of?

- ***Fears from the wider world***
  - o *Stylist* magazine – "87% of British women experience sexism at work, says Stylist study":
    *https://www.stylist.co.uk/stylist-live/stylist-study-reveals-sexism-still-rife-in-the-workplace-women-feminism-inequality-gender-pay-gap-corbyn/8611*.
- ***Breathing and mindfulness***
  - o Karen Farrell:
    *https://uk.linkedin.com/in/karenfarrellmindfulness*.
  - o Calm app: *https://www.calm.com/*.
  - o Yoga with Adriene: *https://yogawithadriene.com/*
  - o Pilates with Laura:
    *https://www.instagram.com/pilates.with.laura/*

## Chapter 6: Breaking out the influencing guns

- Chartwell – "Positive Power and Influence": *https://www.chartwell-learning.com/positive-power-and-influence/*.
- Radical Candor: *https://www.radicalcandor.com/*.
- DDI – STAR Method: *https://www.ddiworld.com/solutions/behavioral-interviewing/star-method*.
- *Co-creating value in organizations with ITIL 4: a guide for consultants, executives and managers*: *https://www.amazon.co.uk/Co-creating-value-organizations-ITIL-consultants/dp/0113318510*.

## Chapter 7: Breaking down the barriers – Shattering limits

- *Mental-health challenges*
  - Mind: *https://www.mind.org.uk/*.
  - ANDYSMANCLUB: *https://andysmanclub.co.uk/*.
  - Samaritans: *https://www.samaritans.org/how-we-can-help/contact-samaritan/*.
  - World Health Organisation: *https://www.who.int/health-topics/mental-health*.

## Chapter 8: Breaking down the barriers – Defying the norm

- *Workplace inequality*
  - Harvard Business School: Working Knowledge – "Breaking Through the Self-Doubt That Keeps Talented Women from Leading":

> *https://www.library.hbs.edu/working-knowledge/breaking-through-the-self-doubt-that-keeps-talented-women-from-leading*

- ***Limited support networks***
  - TechHer: *https://techherng.com*.
  - SheCodes: *https://www.shecodes.io/*.
  - *it*SMF UK: *https://www.itsmf.co.uk/women-in-itsm-2025/*.
  - Women in Tech: *https://www.womenintech.co.uk/*.
  - British Computer Society (BCS): *https://www.bcs.org/*.
  - *it*SMF UK: *https://www.itsmf.co.uk/*.
  - Association for Women in Computing: *https://www.awc-hq.org/home.html*.
  - Service Desk Institute (SDI): *https://www.servicedeskinstitute.com/*.
  - Open Service Community: *https://openservicecommunity.com/*.
  - Scopism SIAM Community: *https://www.scopism.com/siam-community/*.
  - Reed's Women in Technology community: *https://resources.reed.com/women-in-technology-mentoring-programme*.
- ***Sexual harassment and discrimination***
  - *Allyship Actually: https://allyshipactually.com/*.

## Chapter 9: Investing in the bank of you

- ***Finding your passion(s)***
  - PPD Studios: *https://www.ppdstudios.co.uk/*

*Appendix: Sources, resources and where to find support*

- **Personal development**
  - ○ Simon Sinek's books:
    *https://simonsinek.com/books/*.
  - ○ Brené Brown's books:
    *https://brenebrown.com/books-audio/*.
  - ○ Getting Things Done GTD®:
    *https://gettingthingsdone.com/*.
  - ○ Forbes's best self-help books:
    *https://www.forbes.com/sites/entertainment/article/best-self-help-books/*.
  - ○ High Performance podcast:
    *https://www.thehighperformancepodcast.com/*.
  - ○ The Diary of a CEO:
    *https://stevenbartlett.com/doac/*.
  - ○ Mel Robbins's podcast:
    *https://www.melrobbins.com/podcast/*.
  - ○ Alex Cooper presents Call Her Daddy:
    *https://www.youtube.com/@callherdaddy/videos*.
  - ○ EQ-i 2: *https://www.eitrainingcompany.com/eq-i/*.
  - ○ Insights: *https://www.insights.com/*.
  - ○ Myers-Briggs: *https://www.myersbriggs.org/*.
- **Mentoring**
  - ○ BCS: *https://www.bcs.org/membership-and-registrations/become-a-member/mentoring/*
  - ○ Reed's Women in Technology Programme:
    *https://resources.reed.com/women-in-technology-mentoring-programme*.
  - ○ *it*SMF:
    *https://www.itsmf.co.uk/services/mentorship/*.

- ***Coaching***
  - Samantha Harman: *https://www.thestyleeditor.co.uk/*.
  - Lucy Grimwade: *https://www.lightsparkgroup.com/*.
  - Hanna Zaxmy: *https://migmatit.se/en/*.

# FURTHER READING

GRC Solutions is the world's leading publisher for governance and compliance. Our industry-leading pocket guides, books and training resources are written by real-world practitioners and thought leaders. They are used globally by audiences of all levels, from students to C-suite executives.

Our high-quality publications cover all IT governance, risk and compliance frameworks and are available in a range of formats. This ensures our customers can access the information they need in the way they need it.

Other books you may find useful include:

- *Allyship Actually – Why it's 'We' and not 'Me'* by Lucy Grimwade and David Barrow, *www.itgovernance.co.uk/shop/product/allyship-actually-why-its-we-and-not-me*

- *An Education in Service Management – A guide to building a successful service management career and delivering organisational success* by David Barrow, *www.itgovernance.co.uk/shop/product/an-education-in-service-management-a-guide-to-building-a-successful-service-management-career-and-delivering-organisational-success*

- *Well-being in the Workplace – A guide to resilience for individuals and teams* by Sarah Cook, *www.itgovernance.co.uk/shop/product/well-being-in-*

*the-workplace-a-guide-to-resilience-for-individuals-and-teams*

For more information on GRC Solutions and IT Governance™, a GRC Solutions Company as well as branded publishing services, please visit *https://www.itgovernance.co.uk/*.

## Branded publishing

Through our branded publishing service, you can customise our publications with your organisation's branding. For more information, please contact:

*clientservices-uk@grcsolutions.io*

## Related services

GRC Solutions offers a comprehensive range of complementary products and services to help organisations meet their objectives.

For a full range of resources, please visit *www.itgovernance.co.uk*.

## Training services

GRC Solutions' training programme is built on our extensive practical experience designing and implementing management systems based on ISO standards, best practice and regulations.

Our courses help attendees develop practical skills and comply with contractual and regulatory requirements. They also support career development via recognised qualifications.

Learn more about our training courses and view the full course catalogue at *www.itgovernance.co.uk/training.*

**Professional services and consultancy**

We are a leading global consultancy of IT governance, risk management and compliance solutions. We advise organisations around the world on their most critical issues and present cost-saving and risk-reducing solutions based on international best practice and frameworks.

We offer a wide range of delivery methods to suit all budgets, timescales and preferred project approaches.

Find out how our consultancy services can help your organisation at

*www.itgovernance.co.uk/consulting*.

**Industry news**

Want to stay up to date with the latest developments and resources in the IT governance and compliance market? Subscribe to our Security Spotlight newsletter and we will send you mobile-friendly emails with fresh news and features about your preferred areas of interest, as well as unmissable offers and free resources to help you successfully start your project: *www.itgovernance.co.uk/security-spotlight-newsletter.*

EU for product safety is Stephen Evans, The Mill Enterprise Hub, Stagreenan, Drogheda, Co. Louth, A92 CD3D, Ireland. (servicecentre@itgovernance.eu)

www.ingramcontent.com/pod-product-compliance
Lightning Source LLC
Chambersburg PA
CBHW042313210326
41599CB00038B/7117